YORK NOTES

Dubliners

James Joyce

Notes by John Brannigan

Longman   York Press

YORK PRESS
322 Old Brompton Road, London SW5 9JH

ADDISON WESLEY LONGMAN LIMITED
Edinburgh Gate, Harlow,
Essex CM20 2JE, United Kingdom
Associated companies, branches and representatives throughout the world

First published 1998

ISBN 0-582-32911-6

Designed by Vicki Pacey, Trojan Horse, London
Maps by Celia Hart
Phototypeset by Gem Graphics, Trenance, Mawgan Porth, Cornwall
Colour reproduction and film output by Spectrum Colour
Produced by Addison Wesley Longman China Limited, Hong Kong

CONTENTS

Y

PART ONE

INTRODUCTION

HOW TO STUDY A SHORT STORY

Studying on your own requires self-discipline and a carefully thought-out work plan in order to be effective.

- By definition, the short story is condensed. Therefore it requires a lot of careful unpacking.
- You will need to read the short story several times. After the second or third reading, write down any features (language, images, characters, settings, ideas) you find interesting or unusual.
- Think about how the story is narrated. From whose point of view are the events described?
- Do the characters develop? Which characters do you like or dislike? Does some change to a character act as a turning point?
- Does the story have a plot? Is the arrangement of events in time significant? What is the effect of the ending? Is the action completed and closed or left incomplete and open?
- What part does setting play in the story?
- Are words, images and incidents repeated so as to give the work a pattern?
- Is there anything special about the kind of language the writer has chosen?
- What do you think the story is about? What are its central themes or ideas? Does the story present a moral and just world?
- Do not consider the story in isolation. Can you compare and contrast the story with any other work by the same author or with any other text that deals with the same theme?
- Every argument you make about the story must be backed up with details and quotations that explore its language and organisation.
- Always express your ideas in your own words.

This York Note offers an introduction to *Dubliners* and cannot substitute for close reading of the text and the study of secondary sources.

There are many reasons to enjoy and celebrate James Joyce's *Dubliners*. To begin with, there are few collections of short stories in English which are so sharply focused on developing a handful of themes in so consistent and methodical a fashion from the first story to the last. Joyce designed *Dubliners* as a collection, and for each story to be read in relation to the others. The despair of the boy at the end of 'Araby' is made more poignant with the recognition which comes with reading each subsequent story that his despair will turn to frustration, and finally to resignation. Joyce set out to represent the paralysis of the will which was besetting his home city of Dublin and all of its inhabitants, and he made this theme the focus of each of the stories in the collection. For this reason, *Dubliners*, like few other collections of short stories, has a central focus and moral, to which each story contributes in its own way. So, although each story can be read individually, and enjoyed on its own merits, there is also a great deal of pleasure and insight to be gained from reading the collection as a whole.

Dubliners is also a remarkable combination of humour and observation. The dialogue, characterisation and narration of each of the stories is frequently entertaining, poking fun at some characters for their curious expressions, and making **ironic** the serious gestures of sombre characters. While having fun, *Dubliners* is also a study of human behaviour, communication and values. It follows the lives of people who search in vain for happiness in money, or who live out their disappointments and frustrations through others, or who bolster false images of themselves, only to be further aggrieved when those images are deflated. The stories are brief encounters with a handful of characters and situations, situations which often appear trivial or meaningless, but they allow us to see a world of hopes, dreams, failures, corruption, bewilderment, anger, greed, ambition, desire and embarrassment. Joyce exhibits the whole gamut of human emotions and conceits in the space of fifteen short stories and yet, at the same time, has written those stories with the brevity and economy necessary for the short story form.

Dubliners describes and brings to life the city of Dublin at the beginning of the twentieth century, and each of the stories is set against a background of real streets, shops and icons which make up the architecture of the city. The collection is, for this reason, an intriguing mix of social **realism** and the literary imagination. It rewards the reader on many levels, whether in a cursory reading or after lengthy, careful research. Perhaps the most noteworthy achievement of *Dubliners*, as Colin MacCabe has suggested (Colin MacCabe, *James Joyce and the Revolution of the Word*, Macmillan, 1979, pp. 28–37), is its openness to very different readers. People with little or no knowledge of Dublin, literature or **symbolism** may find stories which are captivating and rewarding, just as much as scholars may gain pleasure from tracing the dense literary and theological allusions, or the map of Dublin which Joyce draws through his stories.

As a text to be studied and analysed, *Dubliners* presents the student with some challenging and tantalising questions. If *Dubliners* has a central focus and moral, why did Joyce write it as a collection of stories, each with different characters and situations, and not as a novel? What is Joyce's attitude to Dublin and Ireland? Is he sick of it, like Gabriel Conroy? Or is he obsessed with and enchanted by it? Is Joyce the impartial observer and narrator of these incidents and characters, or does he intervene, offering his own views and solutions? What are the **epiphanies**, or revelations of truth, in *Dubliners* and what roles do they play? Are Joyce's stories offering political views? Or ethical views? Do the stories present the reader with psychological case studies – a woman incapable of escaping, a man consumed by jealous rage, and so on? How does Joyce use **symbols** and images in the stories, and to what purpose? How does Joyce use language, style, characterisation, viewpoint or time pattern in the stories? These questions are discussed and sometimes partly answered in the notes and summaries below, but ultimately many of the most challenging questions and the most rewarding answers will only come with your own close reading and attentive study of the stories of *Dubliners*.

There are other questions which we might ask in relation to Joyce's other works. Was *Dubliners* the text which Joyce used to experiment with the styles and techniques which he would go on to develop and perfect in his later writings? Why did Joyce abandon the short story form after he had completed *Dubliners*? What was the relationship between Joyce's writings and the writings of the Irish Revivalists, such as W.B. Yeats, George Moore and Lady Gregory? But these other questions can only be answered when we have studied the works of Joyce in full and in much detail, which for many scholars, including myself, is always a daunting but very fulfilling task.

PART TWO

SUMMARIES

The date and place of the first publication of each story are indicated in the summaries below. The stories were first published as the Dubliners *collection by Grant Richards in London, 1914. Since 1914,* Dubliners *has been in print almost continuously by various different publishers. The edition used for these Notes is the corrected text with an explanatory note by Robert Scholes, published by Jonathan Cape in 1967.*

THE SISTERS **Publication:** *The Irish Homestead,* **13th August 1904. Pseudonym: Stephen Daedalus.**

The first half of this story is set in the home of the boy-narrator, who lives with his aunt and uncle. The story is chiefly about the relationship between the boy and an old priest, James Flynn, who dies from a stroke. It also concerns the boy's aunt and uncle, the priest's two sisters, Eliza and Nannie, in whose house Father Flynn dies, and old Cotter, a friend of the boy's uncle.

The story begins with the boy pondering the impending death of the priest. When he arrives home he is told that the priest has died, and the boy's uncle tells old Cotter of the relationship between Father Flynn and the boy. This conversation contains some veiled criticisms and suspicions of the priest, and of his influence on the boy, such as Old Cotter telling the boy's uncle: 'I wouldn't like children of mine ... to have too much to say to a man like that' (p. 8).

The second half of the story is set in the home of Flynn's two sisters in Great Britain Street, where the corpse is laid out awaiting the burial ceremony. The boy and his aunt go to the house to pay their respects to the two sisters and to pray over the corpse. There follows a conversation between the boy's aunt and Eliza, in which Eliza is portrayed in a some-what comic role. Her language is often made up of **malapropism** and puns. It could be argued that her role in the story is the most important since it allows us to see the story **parodying** religious attitudes and beliefs.

'The Sisters' sets up a number of recurring themes for the *Dubliners* collection. It begins with the concept of paralysis (see Paralysis in Themes), which was an important feature of all the stories in *Dubliners*, and a central facet of Joyce's view of Dublin as a city. It is narrated from the perspective of a child, and dwells on the formative experience of childhood, a theme which is continued in the three stories following 'The Sisters'. It introduces us to the religious beliefs and debates of late nineteenth century Irish Catholicism, a theme which will form the background of a number of the stories, and which becomes a key theme in 'Grace'. And it is also the first setting of the theme of death, which is the key focus of the final story in the collection, 'The Dead'. We might also note the occasional similarities in language and style between 'The Sisters' and 'The Dead': for instance, 'I felt my soul receding into some pleasant and vicious region' ('The Sisters', p. 9) and 'His soul had approached that region where dwell the vast hosts of the dead' ('The Dead', p. 255).

The boy experiences a degree of ambiguity in his feelings for the priest's death. He admits to feeling 'freed from something by his death' (p. 11), even though he is saddened it. Father Flynn is considered to be a fallen, failed priest, yet he has educated the boy widely in religious matters. These ambiguities suggest complex emotions. They also suggest multiple perspectives in that the priest means different things to different characters. To the church, Flynn might be a failure, but to the boy he represents a world of knowledge and authority. Note also how the priest's character and history are revealed through various perspectives – from the boy, from his uncle and Cotter in conversation, from dreams, from the death notice, and from Eliza and the boy's aunt. This is the beginning of what we will see in all of the stories as the multiple perspectives of Dubliners.

paralysis the narrator is referring here to the condition of the priest after his third stroke, but paralysis is also a recurring theme throughout *Dubliners*. The first sentence of the story sets up the atmosphere of paralysis which Joyce thought pervaded the city of Dublin

gnomon a geometric term for the part of a parallelogram which remains after a similar parallelogram is taken away from one of its corners (from

Euclid, a Greek geometrist of the third century BC). Also, the rod or pin of a sundial

simony the buying and selling of sacred privileges, pardons and absolutions, from Simon Magnus who attempted to buy the power of conferring the Holy Ghost from the Apostles (Acts 8:18–20)

catechism a book containing a summary of the principles of the Christian religion, usually in the form of questions and answers

stirabout porridge or gruel

Rosicrucian the boy's uncle is referring to the boy as a dreamer, but the term derives from the fifteenth century secret order founded by Christian Rosenkreuz. The Rosicrucians were a cultic and mystic order, believing in magical powers

simoniac a priest who practises simony

crape or crêpe: a kind of imitation silk used in black for mourning ribbons, bands and bouquets

R.I.P. Requiescat in Pace. Latin for 'Rest in Peace'. English is used more commonly now, but before 1965 all Catholic ceremonies were in Latin

High Toast a brand of snuff, which is a pulverised tobacco taken by sniffing up the nostrils

mortal or venial Joyce's characters are frequently aware, as would be the case in late nineteenth and early twentieth century Ireland, of the theological debates and doctrines of the Catholic church. Here the narrator is referring to the gradation of sins, some of which are serious wrongs (mortal), which would cast them into eternal damnation if they failed to confess to, and have their sins absolved by, a priest. Less serious sins (venial) might be punished by a stay in purgatory, and could be more easily pardoned in any case

Eucharist the re-enactment in the Christian faith of the ceremony of the last supper, with the priest sharing the bread and wine with his congregation

confessional referring to both the box or compartment in which the priest hears the confessions of sinners, and to the act of the confession itself

Post Office Directory annual publication of the post office giving the names and addresses of residents. It is comparable to current telephone books

Persia Now Iran. It was characteristic in the Victorian period in England to think of the middle east, or the Orient as it was then called, as a place of mystery and the exotic. Because Ireland was a close colony of England, the same cultural assumptions were present in Ireland's attitudes to Persia

altar the table on which the mass, and the Eucharist in particular, is celebrated. It is placed on a stone which has been blessed by a bishop

chalice the cup used for the wine in the Eucharist

did he ... peacefully? the missing word in the narrator's aunt's question is, of course, 'die'. The omission, or **ellipsis**, of the word here is designed to soften the effect of what she is asking. This is known as euphemism, the substitution of a mild or more polite word for something which is shocking or harsh. Death is a word often omitted or substituted – usually replaced with 'passed away', 'gone to rest', or something similarly mild

anointed a sacrament for the dying in which the priest anoints the person with blessed oil, and reads prayers for her/his soul

a beautiful corpse Joyce is parodying attitudes to death in Ireland with this phrase. This occurs with some frequency in his writings. Another renowned example is in his *Ulysses*: 'The Irishman's house is his coffin'

we done all we could the phrase is incorrect grammatically, substituting 'done' for 'did', but Joyce is mimicking the speech patterns and popular syntax of the Irish urban poor in much of the dialogue in *Dubliners*

Freeman's General this refers to the *Freeman's Journal and National Press*, a nationalist paper published in Dublin, particularly noted for its commentaries on religious matters and for its funeral notices

breviary this book briefed the priests on the 'Divine Office' which they were to recite for each day

Irishtown in the east of Dublin and south of the river Liffey, between Sandymount and Ringsend, and next to Dublin bay. A poor quarter of the city which got is name as a ghetto for the Irish during colonial times

new-fangled modern, or new technology

rheumatic Eliza is referring here to 'pneumatic' tyres. The replacement of 'rheumatic' for 'pneumatic' is an example of a **malapropism**. **Malapropism** derives from Mrs Malaprop in Sheridan's play *The Rivals* (1775), and is the device of having a character misconceive or mispronounce a word for comic effect

crossed Eliza means that the priest had bad luck, but the term also puns on Father Flynn's profession. There is **irony** in the story here, for Eliza is seen to be superstitious rather than religious

it contained nothing according to Catholic beliefs, the wine and bread of the Eucharist are transformed into the blood and body of Christ. The spilling of the contents of the chalice is therefore a serious misdemeanour. Eliza attempts to excuse the priest from blame here by first explaining that the chalice might have contained nothing when the priest dropped it, and then suggesting that it was the boy's fault

laughing-like another example of popular syntax, suggesting that the priest was almost laughing, or looked as if he was laughing

AN ENCOUNTER   Publication: Written in 1905. First publication in the first edition of *Dubliners*, 1914.

The story has three parts. In the first part the boy-narrator and his friends, the Dillon brothers and Mahony, are excited by stories of the Wild West, and are inspired to play out and dream of their own adventures and expeditions as a result of reading tales of cowboys and Indians. These adventures are contrasted with the air of proscription and disapproval evident in the attitude of the boys' teacher, Father Butler. The boys dream up a plan to escape school for the following day, but the Dillons do not show up, one because he has a vocation for the priesthood, the other because he is too frightened to play truant.

The second part of the story follows the adventure of the narrator and Mahony, who meet on a bridge over the Royal Canal in the north of the city. They walk along the North Strand Road, then down the Wharf Road, built on a sea wall on Dublin bay, past the Smoothing Iron, a bathing place, and to the quays. Their route takes them along the coast on the north-east side of Dublin. They stop for lunch on the quays, and then cross the mouth of the river Liffey by ferry to south-east Dublin, this takes them across the river Dodder, a tributary of the Liffey, and they stop to lie on the bank of a field.

The third part of the story takes place in the field when a man with a walking stick, shabbily dressed and wearing a jerry hat, approaches them. The man talks to the boys of the weather, then of school and reading, and then of girls. At this point, the narrator suspects the man of being strange, for the man talks of, 'how all girls were not so good as they seemed to be if one only knew' (p. 26). After speaking of his fondness for, 'looking at a nice young girl', the man leaves for a few minutes, and does something at the end of the field. The narrator will not look at what he is doing, even though Mahony expresses surprise and calls the old man, 'a queer old josser' (p. 26). He is presumably masturbating, although we have no way of knowing this.

When the old man returns, Mahony leaves to chase a cat, while the man talks to the narrator of his desire to give young boys, 'a nice warm whipping' (p. 27). The narrator becomes frightened at this point, and finds an excuse to leave. The narrator and Mahony begin to return home, and the narrator is grateful for Mahony's companionship in the aftermath of their encounter with the strange old man.

The story is narrated by a boy, but it is not always clear from what perspective in time it is being narrated. On the one hand, the language used by the narrator adopts the slang and the vocabulary of an adolescent boy, but there are occasional suggestions that the story might be narrated by an older man reflecting on his boyhood. For example, when the narrator describes the old man's hat, he says that the old man, 'wore what we used to call a jerry hat' (p. 24). This line suggests the perspective of an older man, not a boy.

> Like 'The Sisters', 'An Encounter' deals with the passage from childhood to adulthood, from innocence to experience (see Growth and Maturity in Themes). The narrator abandons the world of scholarly knowledge for one day in order to go in search of adventure, and what he finds on this adventure is a sleazy, squalid world of adult desire and corruption. But he also finds a common bond of friendship with Mahony, and regrets having held Mahony in contempt. The narrator and Mahony are on the brink of the adult world, evident in the way that they maintain a form of polite adult conversation with the old man, but they are also removed from this world by their childhood belief in hope and virtue. One approach to the story might then be to regard it as the recognition that hope, virtue and goodness are myths, and that bonds of friendship and trust are the necessary substitutes for virtue in a world where absolute virtue is unattainable.
>
> The story has a religious significance, therefore, in replacing religious ideals, like virtue and truth, with human bonds. Moreover, there is the suggestion in the word 'josser' that the old man is also a priest. The old man's desire to see boys whipped for being interested in girls could mirror the Jesuits' chastisement of boys in school for being interested in adventures. The significance might be that the boys discover a world of excitement and adventure, and are hungry for new forms of knowledge and achievement, only by going outside

the confines of their religious and scholarly instruction. From this approach, the story would be about the damaging effect of education on young people in closing their minds to all varieties of knowledge and experience.

Wild West the western half of the USA, the scene of the cowboy and Indian adventures as told in the genre of 'western' stories which became popular in the late nineteenth century

The Union Jack, Pluck and The Halfpenny Marvel popular magazines which were published first in the 1890s, and aimed to provide instructive role models for boys through stories of adventurers, explorers and travellers

Indian battles mock battles between cowboys or US troops and Native Americans

National School schools for the working classes, which were free and emphasised vocational or trade skills. In contrast, the boys in the story are pupils at Belvedere College, a school run by the Jesuit order, and very fashionable among the wealthy Catholic middle class

miching slang for truancy

pipeclayed a plastic, grey-white clay used for pipemaking, but also used for whitening canvas shoes

mall Charleville Mall, along the Royal Canal in Dublin

gas fun

Bunsen Burner a gas burner used as scientific apparatus, named after R.W. Bunsen

funk flunk, fail or panic

a bob and a tanner slang for a shilling and a sixpence, pre-metric money. Twenty shillings formed a pound, and sixpence was half a shilling

Swaddlers! a derogatory Irish Catholic term for Protestants, particularly Wesleyan Methodists, that refers to Catholic perceptions of the Protestant faiths as being restrictive, or swaddled

Smoothing Iron a bathing place on Dublin bay, so called for the shape of a rock which took the shape of a smoothing iron, and formed the diving platform for bathers

how many how many strokes of the pandybat, or cane, he would get

skit slang for adventure or fun

jerry hat stiff felt hat

Thomas Moore Irish poet and songwriter, 1779–1852, famous for his drawing room melodies and patriotic songs

Walter Scott Scottish poet and novelist, 1771–1832, author of many historical novels

Lord Lytton English novelist and MP, 1803–73, author of popular historical novels

totties slang for girlfriends, possibly derived from Hottentot; also a high class prostitute

a queer old josser josser is slang for man. It can also mean worshipper or priest of a god. It suggests deviating from a sexual norm, a sense which might be supported by the lack of clarity about what Mahony sees the old man doing, and the man's excessive talk about whipping young boys which follows

ARABY   Publication: Written in 1905. Published first in *Dubliners*, 1914.

The narrator of the story is a boy infatuated with the sister of a friend, Mangan. In the opening of the story he is describing the typical play of himself and his friends, and describing their surroundings in north-east Dublin. The boy, who lives with his uncle and aunt in North Richmond Street, watches Mangan's sister from afar, and is filled with the longing and despair of infatuation. He thinks of her, follows her, and watches her movements in adoration, but never speaks to her. Then one day, she asks him if he is going to the Araby bazaar, and explains that she cannot go as she is obliged to go to a retreat run by her convent. The narrator promises to go and to bring her something as a gift from the bazaar.

Throughout the story the language of adoration and romance, with words such as 'sensation', 'my heart', 'my bosom', and allusions to the romanticism of 'Arabia' in English writing of the nineteenth century, are contrasted with the language of materialism and money, such as the words 'marketing', 'bargaining' and 'shop-boys'. Mrs Mercer, the pawnbroker's widow, represents the materialistic contrast to the narrator's spirituality in her quest to acquire used stamps which she is accumulating for 'some pious purpose' (p. 33). Conventional spirituality, through religious institutions like church charities, is a crude materialism in contrast to the sensuous spirituality of the narrator's adoration of Mangan's sister, which is described in exalted romantic terms.

The narrator waits at home for his uncle to arrive and give him money for the bazaar, but his uncle forgets and arrives late, leaving the boy very little time to go to the bazaar. He takes a train from the north-east of the city to the south-east, where the bazaar is held. There, rather than a celebration of everything exotic, sensuous and romantic which he expects to find, he finds a world of trade, commerce and vulgarity, devoid of romance. In the emptiness of the bazaar, which is almost closed and is cast into darkness, he sees his own infatuation as empty too.

In 'Araby', it might be argued, we see another ideal or myth dispelled. If virtue was found to be impossible in 'An Encounter', in 'Araby' the narrator finds that the pursuit of the ideal of love – real romance and sensuousness – is nothing but vanity. Although this may be the revelation which the narrator comes to at the end of the pursuit, the experience of adoration and love is real enough for him. He experiences leaps of the heart, bursts of tears, and feels his body as a harp, 'and her words and gestures were like fingers running upon the wires' (p. 31). This is juxtaposed with images and signs of a shabby realism surrounding him, the street-singers, suggestions of sexual innuendoes and signs of materialism. Although he surrounds himself in 'Eastern enchantment', Araby turns out to be depressingly crass in its use of exotic symbolism as a way of marketing cheap and bawdy wares.

There are, then, two awakenings in this story. The first is the narrator's awakening sexuality and sense of desire. The second is the narrator's realisation that desire can be illusory, and that not everything that looks or sounds exotic and romantic proves to be the real thing. Note the use of language to evoke the feeling of emptiness, futility and waste in the story – words like 'rusty', 'useless', 'waste-room', 'littered' and 'straggling' in the opening, for instance. Language is also used to assign personality or individuality to things – the houses 'gazed at one another with brown imperturbable faces' (p. 29) is an example (see Language and Style in Techniques). This suggests the significance of places and surroundings, and of the city itself as a living being, in the lives of Joyce's characters.

Araby Araby was a bazaar organised in aid of the Jervis Street Hospital in May 1894, and advertised as a 'Grand Oriental Fête'. Araby was a poetic name for

Arabia, and the fête appears to be part of the late Victorian dream of the romanticism, sensuality and exoticism of the Orient

blind North Richmond street was a cul-de-sac, located in the north-east area of the city

Christian Brothers a teaching order founded in Waterford in 1802, which ran schools at low fees for boys, emphasising trade and practical skills

The Abbot Walter Scott's novel from 1820 which idealises Mary Queen of Scots

The Devout Communicant Pacificus Baker's religious tract from 1813 on the Eucharist

The Memoirs of Vidocq François-Jules Vidocq began a career as a criminal, and then became a detective, and his memoirs tell of his adventures on both sides of the law. His memoirs appeared in 1828

the areas sunken spaces between the basement and the street allowing for access, light and ventilation

Mangan's sister it is possible that Joyce is using the name of Mangan here to remind the reader of James Clarence Mangan, 1803–1849, an Irish poet famous for his poems of unrequited love, and romantic agony

come-all-you ballads, initially those which began with these words, but later came to refer to ballads and popular songs in general

O'Donovan Rossa nationalist hero and Fenian leader, Jeremiah O'Donovan, 1831–1915, who came from Ross Carberry in Cork, and who acquired the name Dynamite Rossa for his violent attempts to win Ireland's independence in the 1850s and 1860s

chalice the cup used in the Eucharist ceremony, but here also perhaps the 'Holy Grail' chalice of Arthurian legend

retreat a time for reflection and religious contemplation organised by a religious order

Freemason affair the Freemasons are a secret society of men, and in Ireland were perceived to be anti-Catholic and pro-establishment. The aunt may be confusing the Araby bazaar with a Freemason exhibition organised in 1892, as noted by Gifford in *Joyce Annotated: Notes for* Dubliners *and* A Portrait (University of California Press, 1982), p. 47

some pious purpose that is, to go to a religious charity

night of Our Lord a convention of the time to refer to this night

The Arab's Farewell a poem by Caroline Norton, 1808–77

florin two shillings

ARABY continued

Café Chantant literally 'singing café', providing refreshments and
entertainment
salver a tray or platter, usually made of gold, silver, brass or some plating

EVELINE   Publication: First published in *The Irish Homestead*, 10th September 1904.

'Eveline' begins with the heroine sat still beside a window, looking out at
the world passing, and remembering childhood games. Whereas the first
three stories of *Dubliners* were about the life of a child, or young adolescent,
'Eveline' deals with a young woman caught between the obligation to look
after her father and the chance to escape to a new life with her boyfriend,
the sailor, Frank. At home she faces the prospect of her father's violence.
There is the suggestion that this might involve sexual abuse, as a distinction
is made between the way her father 'used to go for Harry and Ernest', her
brothers, and how he threatens to go for her 'because she was a girl' (p. 39).

With the threat of this violence in mind, Eveline agrees to be Frank's
wife in their new home in Buenos Aires. For much of the story she weighs
up the options of staying in the sterile, hard life looking after her father and
family, or embarking on a new life with Frank. She decides that Frank will
be her salvation, that Frank will give her happiness, and she goes with
him to the port in Dublin to catch the boat out. Once there, however,
Eveline cannot pluck up the courage to leave, and she is helpless to move
off the quayside. She remains trapped in her old life, caught in the paralysis
of the city.

> Like the boys in the three stories preceding 'Eveline' in *Dubliners*,
> Eveline desires escape from the oppressive, paralysed atmosphere of
> Dublin. Eveline is presented with the opportunity to realise the
> dream which the boy in 'The Sisters' has of Persia, the boy in 'An
> Encounter' has of the Wild West, and the boy in 'Araby' has of the
> Orient. The narrator of 'An Encounter' describes the need for escape
> which pervades them all when he says: 'real adventures, I reflected, do
> not happen to people who remain at home: they must be sought
> abroad' (p. 20).
>
> Eveline's choice seems straightforward, between the parochial
> pettiness, the scrimping and labouring, and the threatened violence

and abuse of life in Dublin with her father, and the chance of a new adventurous life in a distant land with her boyfriend. Why, then, does Eveline find it impossible to leave?

Joyce focuses more attention in this story on social environment and economic conditions, enabling us to see the life which is already mapped out for Eveline, of chores and hardships at home, of life with a drunken, abusive father, and the narrowness of her job in the Stores. He also uses language which registers indifference: 'Her father was not so bad then' (p. 37), 'she did not find it a wholly undesireable life' (p. 39). She takes the place of her mother, complete with the prospect of a final lunacy awaiting her.

One possible interpretation is that this environment of duty and responsibility in hardship has removed from Eveline the ability to believe in and carry through her dream of hope, love, escape and freedom. Her environment has sapped her strength, her fortitude, and turns her into the 'helpless animal' which we see at the end of the story. Another interpretation is that in the dichotomy between the known, parochial world of Dublin and the unknown exotic world of Buenos Aires, Eveline makes a choice to stay with the community which she knows, and in that final moment of departure realises that she cannot love a man bound to drift without this kind of community (albeit a harsh, broken community).

Eveline Gifford cites Thomas Moore's 'Eveleen's Bower' as the source of this title, but Terence Brown (notes that a well known Victorian pornographic novel bore the name, in which the heroine has sexual intercourse with her father. Brown suggests mischief in Joyce's choice of title in the Penguin Twentieth-Century Classics edition of *Dubliners*)

keep nix to keep a look-out

Blessed Margaret Mary Alacoque a French nun, 1647–90, who had visions of the Sacred Heart of Jesus. She was beatified in 1864, hence the prefix 'blessed'. The promises mentioned here included comfort, peace in the home, refuge during life, and mercy and salvation in death. Since 1920 she has properly been known as St Margaret Mary Alacoque

the Stores the department store in which Eveline works

down somewhere in the country anywhere in Ireland outside Dublin

the night-boat a boat left Dublin every night for Liverpool

Buenos Ayres capital city of Argentina, and a magnet for European and American adventurers at the turn of the century. Brown also suggests that 'going to Buenos Aires' meant choosing a life of prostitution

The Bohemian Girl a light, three-act opera by Irish composer Michael William Balfe, 1808–70. The opera tells the story of Arlene, a girl of noble stock, kidnapped by gypsies, who grows up to be beautiful and marries an exiled nobleman. Her noble identity is revealed, and the opera ends happily ever after with Arlene enjoying the peaceful gypsy life, and the riches of nobility

the lass that loves a sailor popular song by English songwriter Charles Dibdin, 1745–1814

the Allan Line steamship company based in Liverpool, which operated a service to the Pacific coast of North America via Buenos Aires and Cape Horn

Patagonians in Victorian England the Patagonians, from the southern tip of South America, were imagined as the most fierce, savage people on earth

the old country sentimental phrase used by emigrants and exiles to refer to Ireland

Hill of Howth about nine miles north-east of Dublin, a headland of Dublin bay

Damned Italians Italian immigration into Ireland was very low, making an additional mockery of Eveline's father's outburst

Derevaun Seraun obscure and garbled Gaelic phrase, the meaning of which is not quite clear, but might be 'the end of pleasure is pain', or 'the end of song is raving madness'. The latter would make sense in view of Eveline's mention of her mother's, 'life of commonplace sacrifices closing in final craziness' (p. 41)

North Wall the dock on the north bank of the Liffey in the east of the city from which the night-boat for Liverpool departed

AFTER THE RACE   Publication: First published in *The Irish Homestead*, 17th December 1904.

A 26 year old Dublin man, Jimmy Doyle, socialises with three acquaintances: the rich Frenchman, Charles Ségouin, Ségouin's cousin, André Rivière, and a huge Hungarian, Villona. They have spent the day at the Gordon-Bennett Automobile race, and the story begins with the four men travelling in Ségouin's car into Dublin. Although not all of the men are rich, their exuberance, humour, and the fact that they are travelling in a car is contrasted with the 'gratefully oppressed' Dubliners whom they pass. They live a life of affluence and excess, driving in cars, eating in expensive hotels, and gambling on cards.

The main character, Jimmy Doyle, is not always very comfortable with this life, and there are signs of foreboding in the story which point towards its sombre ending. Doyle wants to fit in with the life of international playboys like Ségouin, but something is holding him back from doing so. His father, a wealthy butcher, approves of his aspirations and his rich friends, referring to Ségouin as someone 'well worth knowing' (p. 45). Like Dublin, struggling against colonial domination to be a capital city, Doyle is too keen to get on with rich friends, to socialise with the wealthy for the sake of improving his social position, to be an international playboy himself. This might be a story as much about the international pretensions of Dublin as it is about the wealthy pretensions of Doyle. If so, it is a cautionary tale, for the story ends with Doyle's dawning realisation that he cannot keep up with the fast living and rich excesses of his wealthy friends.

> The language and structure of the story are constructed to provide a rhythm of mood swings. Joyce repeatedly inflates and then deflates the mood of the story by using words like 'happy', 'cheer', 'humour', 'rich', and 'excited' in close proximity, and then deflating the mood by introducing contrasting phrases: 'unfortunately, very poor', 'a curious feeling of disappointment', 'there was even danger of personal spite', and 'the heaviest losers'. The buoyant, happy words maintain an atmosphere of wealth, enjoyment and excess, while at several points in the story the use of cautionary or sombre phrases puncture the happiness of the men with a feeling that something is very wrong, at least for Doyle.

> The story is structured by a series of climaxes and anti-climaxes, which resolve themselves into Doyle's moment of awakening at the end of the story. Daybreak, with its grey light, is a warning for Doyle that everything he has aspired towards is flimsy and superficial. In one card game, he has lost his wealth and ends up in debt to the winners. The story sets up **allegories** between individuals and nations (with Doyle representing Ireland, Ségouin France, Routh England and so on), and thus the story seems to cast some criticisms on Ireland's rich for throwing their money at continental pretensions, and being

complicit in the oppression of Ireland's poor. The rich Irish change their politics to fit in with the international playboy set. Doyle's father, we are told, used to be a nationalist, but 'had modified his views early' (p. 45), while Jimmy Doyle has been sent to Cambridge to fit in with the English aristocracy and the European élite.

The story is full of the outward trappings of wealth — automobiles, electric candle-lights, yachts and cultural conversation. But in the background of the story we can see the 'gratefully oppressed', ironically cheering on the wealthy European powers. What is it we see at the end of the story in Doyle's sense of foreboding? Does he realise that he has tried to play a game which is far beyond his means and abilities? Does he feel that he has been easy prey for rich strangers who have 'wealth and industry' behind them? The end of the story is inconclusive, but it does imply that Doyle and Ireland are being manipulated and duped in their race to conform to European expectations and capitalist ideals.

After the Race the story refers to the fourth annual Gordon-Bennett Automobile race, held in Ireland on 2nd July 1903. The race took cars from France, Germany, Britain and the USA on a 370 mile course through counties in the east midlands, mostly Kildare. The outcome of the race is indicated correctly in Joyce's story: a German car first, driven by a Belgian, Jenatzy, followed by two French cars in second and third

the Naas Road between Dublin and Kildare, to the south-west of Dublin

Inchicore on the south-west border of Dublin city

their friends, the French the Irish may have identified with the French for two reasons. In the first place France, like Ireland, was a predominantly Catholic country. Secondly, French troops had come to the assistance of the Irish in their rebellion against British rule in 1798, and Ireland aspired to become independent from Britain and to form a state based on the same ideal of Republican government as France had created in 1789. When a small French force came to the aid of Irish revolutionaries in 1798, they won a short-lived victory over the English in a battle called the 'Races of Castlebar'. Like the Irish cheering the French cars in the story, the Irish cheered the French victory in 1798, but the title of the story is directing us to the aftermath, which was English victory and domination

Gallicism French mode of being, or French spirit

advanced Nationalist supporter of the Irish Nationalist Party which fought political campaigns for a separate parliament and legislative power for Ireland

Kingstown originally, and now named, Dun Laoghaire, but named Kingstown after 1821 to mark King George IV's visit to Ireland in that year. It was, and still is, the main port of departure from Ireland to Holyhead in Wales. In 1903 it was a mainly Protestant town, with very Anglophile characteristics

police contracts government contracts to supply food to barracks and prisons

Dublin University Trinity College, Dublin, which had acquired a reputation for an Anglo-Protestant orientation

a term at Cambridge only available to wealthy families, it was common for young gentlemen to spend some time at Cambridge or Oxford without taking a degree, in order to socialise

Dame Street, Bank, Grafton Street all fashionable parts of the wealthier south-side of Dublin

northward going northward takes them over the Liffey to the poorer north-side of the city

electric candle-lamps indicating an affluent hotel

English madrigal ... old instruments at this time, there was a revival of interest among intellectuals in the musical fashions of Renaissance England, which included the madrigal, a 5 or 6 part polyphonic song, and in Renaissance musical instruments like the lute, cornet and viol

the mask of a capital in 1903, of course, Dublin was only a provincial capital in the United Kingdom of Great Britain and Ireland. London was the administrative and political capital. The mention of Dublin wearing the mask of a capital suggests the aspiration among the Irish for independence, and the pretension to look like a European capital

Stephen's Green fashionable park on the south-side of the city

Cadet Roussel ... Ho! a French marching song of the 1790s, and its refrain

The Belle of Newport Newport, Rhode Island in the USA has the reputation of a haven for the American rich

TWO GALLANTS   **Publication: Written in 1906. First published in**
                 Dubliners, **1914.**

Corley and Lenehan are the two gallants of the title, but the gallantry referred to is **ironic**. This story features much walking, especially for Lenehan, who walks almost the very same route twice. Corley is depicted as a libertine or seducer, full of talk about his exploits with women, and Lenehan is the leech who hangs on his every word and replies with flattering remarks. They talk about Corley's relationship with a girl, who he is about to meet, and Lenehan is anxious that Corley obtain from the girl something which remains unnamed and elusive.

Corley meets the girl and takes her on a tram out to Donnybrook, but the story focuses on Lenehan who stays in the city centre and occupies the time before meeting up with Corley again by walking back over their route and stopping for 'a plate of peas' and 'a bottle of ginger beer' (p. 61). He ponders his life, and his age, now thirty, and wonders if he will find a simple girl with money to marry. Lenehan goes to the arranged meeting point, and watches Corley and the girl return. The girl, a servant, goes into the house of her service and returns, handing something to Corley. Corley then leaves, and Lenehan follows him, almost getting angry when Corley will not tell him if he has been successful or not. Corley then shows Lenehan a gold sovereign, but the story does not explain or even suggest how Corley earned the money, or why the girl gave it to him.

> Although the characters are in their early thirties, this story belongs to the adolescent stories of *Dubliners*, because the characters refuse to grow old, trapped in the same paralysis which Joyce saw as central to Dublin. The 'two gallants' of the title are depicted as parasites – Corley on the women whom he seduces and from whom he somehow obtains money, Lenehan on his friends, bartenders, and indeed on Corley.

> The meanings of the story are difficult to grasp, largely because of the omission of explanations of the mysterious transaction which takes place between the girl and Corley. But Donald Torchiana (see Further Reading) suggests that the story is an **allegorical** tale about the Anglo-Irish Ascendancy, and the culture of parasitism and exploitation which they bred in Ireland. The evidence to support this view can be found in the references to the Ascendancy in the Kildare Street Club, and in the place names (such as Rutland Square, Shelbourne Hotel and Hume Street) which owe their names to Ascendancy figures. It is also possible to see the girl as a symbol of Ireland, as was common at the time in Yeats's use of Kathleen ni Houlihan, and the Poor Old Woman, a beautiful woman turned

half-prostitute, representing Ireland's depraved condition under colonial rule. This idea of Ireland prostituted by her English conquerors is a possible interpretation of the image of the harp being plucked heedlessly for strangers by her master's hands, near to the Kildare Street club:

> He plucked at the wires heedlessly, glancing quickly from time to time at the face of each new-comer and from time to time, wearily also, at the sky. His harp too, heedless that her coverings had fallen about her knees, seemed weary alike of the eyes of strangers and of her master's hands. (pp. 57–8)

The image of an Irish harp with 'her' clothes 'about her knees' suggests the state of sexual and moral degradation to which colonisation has brought the country.

takes the biscuit slang for the best, or wins the prize

recherché rare, or specially chosen

racing tissues racing forms, information about horse and dog races

Waterhouse's Clock a jewellers on Dame Street, south of the Liffey

the canal the Grand canal on the south-side

a slavey a general maid or servant

the real cheese slang for the real thing

the family way meaning pregnant

up to the dodge slang for she knows what to do, in this case, how to avoid pregnancy

Pim's a retail chain of upholstery, furniture and textiles, highly respected and trusted in Dublin

hairy slang for shrewd, or slippery

about town unemployed, but scraping a living

the hard word disagreeable information on the available job

Florentines citizens of Florence, Italy, who pronounce *c* as *h*, so making Corley pronounced Horely. Perhaps a pun, whorely, is intended here

Lothario from *The Fair Penitent* (1703), by Nicholas Rowe, 1674–1718, Lothario is a libertine or seducer

on the turf slang for prostitute. Earl Street was next to the red light district

Ecod! garbled version of 'by God', or 'ye Gods'; a simple exclamation

the club the Kildare Street Club, an exclusive conservative club, synonymous with Anglo-Irish and Protestant upper-class power

His harp ... strangers possibly a reference to conventional Irish metaphors for Ireland (the harp) and the coloniser, England (strangers). Harps and strangers were used frequently in Gaelic and Irish poetry to refer subversively and secretly to the nationalist war against England

Silent, O'Moyle part of the first line of Thomas Moore's 'Song of Fionnuala', which contains the line: 'Still in her darkness doth Erin lie sleeping'

get inside me meaning, are you trying to be me? or, you're getting too close, a feeling which the leech-like Lenehan must often provoke

stems upwards according to the etiquette of the time, the stems ought to be worn downwards, indicating lack of sophistication

Shelbourne Hotel very fashionable hotel on St Stephen's Green (see Maps)

curates literally clergymen who assist a vicar in celebrating mass, but used here as slang for bartenders

Three halfpence a cheap meal, indicating that the establishment is a lower-class lunch counter

pulling the devil by the tail scraping a living, or living close to poverty

the ready money

Egan's Egan's pub, The Oval, on Abbey Street Middle, just north of the Liffey

College of Surgeons on St Stephen's Green

the area below the street, in front of the basement of a house

A woman the same woman who has been with Corley. She has evidently entered the building by the basement and come out again through the street level door

small gold coin one pound, a gold sovereign, which Gifford estimates as a considerable sum, about 6 or 7 weeks wages for the girl. This might indicate that she has stolen the money

THE BOARDING HOUSE

Publication: Written in 1905. First published in *Dubliners*, 1914.

The story begins with Mrs Mooney who marries the foreman of her father's butcher's shop, but finds that her husband is a drunkard and squanders their money. She gets a separation order from her husband, sanctioned by the church, and sets up a boarding house in north-east Dublin, taking in working-class tourists and low class entertainers. Mrs Mooney's daughter, Polly, flirts with the young men who are lodgers at the boarding house, but

Mrs Mooney believes that there is no harm in the flirting, and nothing serious going on between Polly and the men. But there is a suggestion that the boarding house acquires a reputation as a brothel as a result: the fact that the landlady is called 'The Madam' by the young men, that she permits the flirtations of her daughter with the young men, and that Polly is described as a 'perverse madonna' (p. 67), suggesting a corrupted beauty, might support this view of the story.

Polly does have a relationship with one of the young men, Mr Doran, and it is implied that Polly is pregnant. Mrs Mooney decides that the proper reparation for this misdemeanour under her roof is to have Mr Doran propose marriage to her daughter. It is possible to read this outcome as the deliberate strategy of Mrs Mooney from the beginning, since she permits the flirting, and sees Polly as a considerable asset in keeping the young men interested in staying at the boarding house. And Mr Doran's anxieties about Polly's lower-class manners and speech may imply that the match is a beneficial one for Polly.

The story concludes with Polly looking forward to a life with Mr Doran, although we know nothing more than the fact that Mr Doran has spoken to Mrs Mooney and now wants to speak to Polly. This probably suggests a proposal of marriage, and the trap is hinted in the final line: 'Then she remembered what she had been waiting for' (p. 75). The action of the story takes place entirely indoors.

'The Boarding House' is interesting for the section of Dublin life which it portrays. Almost all of the people in the story are agents for something else, or are the guarantors of a transaction. They are neither producers nor consumers, but are in a kind of middle state between. The boarding house is neither home nor homelessness, but something temporary and transitory.

'The Madam' is a host or agent who guarantees either accommodation or sex, depending on the sense of the word, in exchange for money. Mrs Mooney's son, Jack, works for a commission agent, who handles other people's business for money. Her daughter, Polly, works briefly for a corn-factor, another middleman agency, which guarantees an exchange of corn for commission. And her husband works as a sheriff's man, running errands, and therefore making transactions possible. The artistes sell some form of entertainment, which may be seedy or suspect also. Mr Doran, too, works for a wine merchant, buying and selling wines. All of the characters, then, with the possible exception of Doran, work in a peripheral, suspect sphere of lower middle class business. They form the seedy, squalid margins of commerce, 'shabby' and 'disreputable'.

According to this interpretation of the story, the seedy world of commerce inhabits every aspect of the lives of Dubliners. The implied marriage of Polly and Mr Doran is conceived from the beginning as a commercial transaction in which Mr Doran is made to pay reparations for his sexual liaisons with Polly. So too, the religious attitudes of both Mr Doran and Mrs Mooney are laced with the language of business. Mrs Mooney saves time (and money) by going to a short mass, especially geared to improving the efficiency of church-going. Mr Doran attends confession, and is glad to find 'a loophole of reparation' (p. 71). Marriage is the price which Doran must pay in order to keep his job, since 'Dublin is such a small city: everyone knows everyone else's business' (p. 71). The seedy corruption of this world in which everyone knows everyone else's business, and in which every aspect of life becomes a business transaction, is another dimension of the paralysis and entrapment of Dublin life.

the pledge an oath to God, organised by Catholic societies, to give up drinking alcohol

a separation a legal separation of marriage partners by the Catholic church, which would not sanction divorce

a sheriff's man an errand boy and small jobs man in the bailiff's office

Liverpool and the Isle of Man there were regular boat services between Dublin and Liverpool which stopped also at the Isle of Man. As a result working class people from those places came to Dublin for holidays

artistes from the music halls often seen as being on the seedy and morally suspect fringes of middle class life

The Madam this title can also mean the manager or hostess of a brothel

favourites and outsiders betting chances or odds on horses

a commission agent in Fleet Street Fleet Street was part of an office district renowned for commissioning agents, who took commission in payment for acting as agents for the business of others (see Maps)

mits slang for hands

corn-factor one who acts as an agent or middleman between the farmer and corn merchants

short twelve at Marlborough Street a short, twenty-minute mass at noon in the Church of the Conception, a Catholic pro-Cathedral, on Marlborough Street, south of Hardwicke Street

the girl has to bear the brunt this would suggest that the girl is pregnant

a good screw good salary

pier-glass a tall mirror between two windows

Reynolds's Newspaper a London Sunday newspaper, which reported on social and political scandals, and had the reputation of upsetting conservatives

a certain fame a reputation, probably that of a Madam, or brothel-keeper

combing-jacket a bathrobe

Bass a strong brown ale, brewed in Staffordshire, England

return-room a small room built onto the wall of a house, sometimes on the first floor landing

A LITTLE CLOUD   Publication: Written in 1906. First published in *Dubliners*, 1914.

Little Chandler, so called for his petite features, meets up with an old friend, Ignatius Gallaher, who has become a successful figure in London newspapers. The story begins with Chandler leaving the King's Inns, where he works as a clerk, and walking south and east to the Burlington Hotel and Bar, known as Corless's, off Dame Street, south of the Liffey (see Maps).

In the course of his walk, he reminds himself of Gallaher's success and of Gallaher's character and life before he left for London. This is contrasted with Chandler's perception of his own life, which has become stagnant and wasteful, and in which he has neglected his enjoyment of poetry and art. Chandler thinks of Gallaher as 'a brilliant figure', whereas Chandler gives 'one the idea of being a little man' (p. 76). He considers that he might have become a famous poet in London, but 'if you wanted to succeed you had to go away. You could do nothing in Dublin' (p. 79). Here, again, is the theme of paralysis in Joyce's portrait of Dublin life.

Chandler meets Gallaher in Corless's Bar, and Gallaher is full of exuberance and humour. Chandler is a more sober, shy character than Gallaher, whose talk of London, Paris and the Continent is both exciting and alienating to Chandler. Gallaher has seen the world, and has led a life more liberated culturally and sexually than Chandler. Conversation turns to Chandler's marriage and his home life, and while Chandler tells Gallaher that he ought to find himself a wife, he envies the freedom of Gallaher's life. Gallaher tells Chandler that married life must 'get a bit stale' (p. 90), and the story moves on to show Chandler at home.

Chandler is left holding the baby while his wife, Annie, is out at the shop. Looking at a photograph of Annie, Chandler thinks that his wife, and indeed his life, lacks passion. He tries to read a poem by Byron, and wonders 'Could he, too, write like that, express the melancholy of his soul in verse?' (p. 92), but the baby begins to cry. Frustrated by what he considers to be the uselessness and the prison of his domestic life, he shouts angrily at the baby, frightening it. At that point, Annie returns, demanding to know what he has done to the child to make it so upset. She caresses the child, and calls it 'Mamma's little lamb of the world' (p. 94), which contrasts with Chandler's feeling that his wife and child have kept him a prisoner from the outside world.

> Joyce contrasts two worlds in this story, the world of domestic, insular and paralysed Dublin and the world of fast-moving, energetic and cosmopolitan London and Europe. Little Chandler desires to belong to the wider, modern world, and begins to despise his life with his family in Dublin.
>
> By juxtaposing Little Chandler with the successful, exuberant Gallaher, Joyce has set up an **antithesis** between the two worlds which they represent. 'A Little Cloud' might refer to the glimmer of hope which Gallaher comes to **symbolise** for Chandler, but the hope is fleeting, for, faced with Gallaher's success and his life of travel and high living, Chandler becomes resentful and bitter about his own life. Chandler's vanity might be seen as part of the cause for his resentment. The language used at the beginning of the story, told from his point of view, indicates his attitude to his fellow Dubliners. They are described as 'minute vermin-like life', and the poor children he meets on his walk are described as 'grimy', and as having 'crawled up', and 'squatted like mice' (p. 77). He feels himself above the parochial, narrow interests of Dublin, and aspires to be a poet, loved by a discerning English readership.

It is the first story in the collection in which married life is the focus, and may represent the theme of maturity, but also entrapment. The 'little cloud' of hope which Gallaher represents in Chandler's life, is also the 'little cloud' of unhappiness which Gallaher casts as a free, fun-loving bachelor over the marriage of Chandler and Annie. Gallaher remains a model of liberty and success to Chandler because he is single, and unburdened by the responsibilities of adult married life.

The theme of entrapment and of the temptation to freedom and passion is present in earlier stories in the *Dubliners* collection also. Notice how Chandler is tempted by the same exoticism – 'dark Oriental eyes' (p. 91) – the same dream of the Orient as the passionate opposite to a dead, dreary Dublin, as is present in 'Araby' and 'Eveline'. Whereas the boy in 'Araby' sees through the illusion of the exoticism marketed in the Araby bazaar, Little Chandler in this story is consumed with too much anger and resentment at his own entrapment, and at the failure of his own dreams, to see through Gallaher's version of an exotic, successful life.

A Little Cloud possibly a reference to the line from I Kings in the Bible, when Elijah's servant says: 'Behold, there ariseth a little cloud out of the sea, like a man's hand' (I Kings 18:44). The Israelites had turned away from God, and Elijah preached that they would be deprived of moisture, dew and rain. The little cloud signified the return of rain to the Israelites when they had renewed their faith in God

the North Wall the port from which passenger ships leave Dublin for England and the Isle of Man

the King's Inns north of the Liffey, the home of Irish legal societies, where barristers are trained, and where law records and libraries are kept

the London Press English newspapers

the old nobility of Dublin had roistered much of the tenement housing in central Dublin at this time had been converted into flats from the large eighteenth century Georgian houses of the Anglo-Irish Ascendency

Corless's Burlington Hotel, Bar and Restaurant, which was known in Joyce's time by the name of its previous owner, Thomas Corless

Atalantas Atalanta was a mythological Greek Princess, who sought to avoid marriage by challenging her suitors to footraces, then overtook them and speared them in the back in passing. Renowned for her agility, she was only tricked into marriage when Hippomenes distracted her by dropping golden apples during a race. Aphrodite, who had given Hippomenes the golden apples, avenged him for his ingratitude by tricking Hippomenes and Atalanta into sacrilege in a temple

Half time slow down, or take a break

my considering cap my thinking cap, or let me think

nearer to London Chandler is travelling south, then east, therefore literally taking him closer to London, but Gallaher now **symbolises** the high life of London for Chandler, and so his meeting with Gallaher is also bringing him nearer metaphorically to London

The Celtic Note Matthew Arnold argued in his book on Celtic Literature from 1867 that Celtic writers represented the artistic, spiritual and feminine side of human nature, whereas English culture was hampered by its materialism and pragmatism. It was part of an argument that England needed to turn to the Celtic fringe to revive the poetical and artistic qualities of English culture

Irish-looking as a result of Arnold's ideas, there was a cult of interest in the stereotypical Celtic poetic sensibility. With his very English-sounding name, Chandler cannot expect to become the object of English cult interest in the Celt. Chandler means 'candle-maker' in English, while his preferred Irish name Malone had a long history in Irish (Gaelic) aristocratic lineage. Chandler also means 'meat-maggot' in Hiberno-English, thereby suggesting that Chandler is part of the 'minute vermin-like life' (p. 77) described early in the story

across the water a euphemism for Britain, over the Irish Sea

Lithia bottled mineral water

the Land Commission the Irish Land Commission Court, which dealt with the transfer of farm properties from Landlords to Tenants. A series of land acts in the late nineteenth century allowed Irish tenants to buy land with the aid of British credit, bringing to an end the system of colonial land ownership which had favoured Anglo-Irish and British landlords, and which had caused vicious political disputes throughout the nineteenth century in Ireland

Booze slang for alcohol

Moulin Rouge famous, risqué music hall in Paris

a catholic gesture a sweeping gesture, indicating a wide area

cocottes French slang for prostitutes

parole d'honneur French for word of honour

a.p. appointment

deoc an doruis not a small drink, as Gallaher believes, but a door-drink, or the last drink before you leave

Bewleys a chain of coffee houses in Dublin, presumably the one on Dame Street, which is closest to him

ten and elevenpence as indicated by Annie's reaction, a very expensive dress

the hire system paying by instalments

Byron's poems Lord Byron, 1788–1824. The poem which Chandler reads is the first stanza of 'On the Death of a Young Lady', which is the first poem in Byron's first collection, 'Hours of Idleness', 1807

That clay ... unfinished line, which reads: 'That clay, where once such animation beam'd'

Lambabaun a term of endearment, meaning lamb-child

COUNTERPARTS   Publication: Written in 1905. First published in *Dubliners*, 1914.

Farrington, the main character of 'Counterparts', is a clerk in the offices of solicitors Crosbie and Alleyne. The story begins in the offices, where Farrington is driven hard by Mr Alleyne to copy out legal reports, and the offices are depicted as oppressive, demoralising surroundings. Feeling under pressure, Farrington slips out of the offices for a drink, and returns to face again the wrath of Mr Alleyne. Notice the words suggesting violence at this point in the story: 'struck', 'blast', 'fist', 'violently'. A confrontation follows between Alleyne and Farrington, in which Alleyne threatens Farrington both with violence and dismissal.

Farrington spends the evening with his friends in a series of pubs. Having raised money by pawning his watch, he spends virtually everything he has buying drinks with his friends. The atmosphere is good humoured and hospitable until Farrington meets with a young woman, who dismissively brushes past him 'and said *O, pardon!* in a London accent' (p. 106). He despairs at not having money, and at buying drinks for a man he dislikes. He is challenged to an arm wrestle by this man, but loses, making him angry and bitter. He makes his way home, full of fury at the upstart who has beaten him in a contest of strength and the young woman who has ignored him.

When he arrives home, his wife has gone out to church and one of his children offers to cook his tea. Farrington notices that the boy has let the fire go out, and beats the boy with a walking stick. The story ends with the boy pleading with his father ('Don't beat me, pa! And I'll ... I'll say a *Hail Mary* for you' p. 109), pledging to say a prayer for him to save his soul.

Farrington in 'Counterparts' might be seen as a slightly older version of Little Chandler in 'A Little Cloud'. Like Chandler, Farrington works as a clerk in a law office, is married in suburban Dublin, and has children. Like Chandler too, Farrington takes out his anger from being trapped in a demoralising job in a narrow, provincial world on his home life. Both Chandler and Farrington are violent towards their children, projecting their resentment of the uselessness and monotony of their working lives on to their families and homes. So too, Weathers and the English girl, both of whom get the better of Farrington, are comparable to Gallaher in 'A Little Cloud' in that they represent the exotic and rich world of London which is beyond the reach of Farrington and Chandler.

The title 'Counterparts' suggests the **antithetical** structure of the story, and indeed many of the stories in *Dubliners*. **Antithesis** is a device which allows Joyce to show the antagonism between two different worlds – in this case, between provincial, paralysed Dublin and the seemingly energetic and uninhibited world outside Ireland – but also the mutual dependence of those opposites. It is only by encountering the other, exotic world that Farrington is able to see the narrowness of his own life.

There are other oppositions in the story. Farrington's daydreaming is contrasted with Alleyne's brutal efficiency, for example. But Farrington acts as the brutal opposite to his son, Tom, who might represent the spirituality which Farrington is missing. In 'Counterparts' Joyce shows a cycle of violence, passed from authoritarian boss on to the worker who takes it home to his son. The city itself seems to breed and thrive on the violence, envy and bitterness which grows from its paralysed condition.

the tube a speaking device for intercommunication
North of Ireland accent often considered abrasive and crass to a southern ear

an order on the cashier authorisation for an advance on wages

the snug a snug is a small room behind a public bar, usually used for private parties, or for after-hours drinking

g.p. a glass (half a pint) of porter

curate bartender

caraway seed the seed of a herb of the carrot family, useful when sucked in concealing the smell of alcohol on the breath

hot punches a hot drink, involving whiskey, hot water, sugar, lemon juice, cloves and cinnamon

manikin dwarf, or derogatory term for small man

touch borrow from

the dart the way to do it

A crown five shillings

the evening editions of the newspapers

he stood Farrington he bought a drink for Farrington

tailors of malt measures of whiskey

the liberal shepherds in the eclogues eclogues are pastoral dialogues, as in Virgil's *Bucolia*. The shepherds are represented as living a simple, idyllic, country life, and are mild-mannered and softly-spoken

naming their poisons a euphemism for naming what drinks they would like

nabs a term of mild mockery, meaning 'know-it-all', or self-appointed authority

bevelled off moved off

the Ballast Office on the south bank of the Liffey, housing the Dublin Port and Docks Board

the Scotch House also on the south bank, a pub owned by James Weir and Co

the Tivoli a place of music hall entertainment, east along the south bank from Scotch House

too Irish an English euphemism for too mad, or too generous. The latter meaning, of generous hospitality, has been adopted in Irish culture

one little tincture a very small drink

small hot specials like hot whiskies or punches, whiskies mixed with sweetened hot water

a sponge slang for one always borrowing or asking for favours

gab slang for snout, or mouth

Pony up pay up

smahan a taste, a tiny drink

> **Sandymount tram** Sandymount was a suburban village a few miles outside Dublin city centre to the east
> **the chapel** a Catholic church
> *Hail Mary* a common Catholic prayer, beseeching the Virgin Mary to 'pray for us sinners'. The child is offering to pray for his father's spiritual salvation, implying the moral and spiritual degradation of his father

C<small>LAY</small>   **Publication: Written in 1905, revised in 1906. First published in *Dubliners*, 1914.**

'Clay' begins in the Dublin by Lamplight Institution, in which Maria, the main character, works in the scullery. It is her evening off, and after she has served tea to the women inmates she makes her way across the city from the south-east to the northern suburb of Drumcondra. She stops in the centre of Dublin to buy treats for the Donnelly family, with whom she will spend the evening. She buys a dozen penny cakes, and for a special treat buys a thick slice of plumcake.

Maria is a shy, diminutive person, and there are numerous suggestions of marriage made by people around her which cause Maria to flush with embarrassment. Joyce also repeats a series of synonyms for smallness, including 'little', 'tiny', 'small', 'tidy', 'diminutive', building up the image of her slight build, but also of her fragility and her very slight presence (see Description, Imagery and Symbolism in Techniques). People seem to pay little attention to her, and to pretend as if she is not there, or that she is too frail to speak for herself. This impression is conveyed more effectively by the fact that she hardly has a line of dialogue until near the end when she sings.

Maria travels on the tram from the city centre to Drumcondra, carrying her parcels with her. On the tram an elderly man, possibly a retired army officer, speaks to her and treats her kindly, which causes her some embarrassment. But when she gets to the Donnelly house, and is greeted by Joe, Mrs Donnelly and the children, she realises that she must have left the plumcake on the tram because of her rush of embarrassment. Maria is quickly the centre of attention for Joe, who treats her like his mother, and for the children who have her join the Hallowe'en games. The story began with the women in the institute joking that Maria would be sure to get the ring from the barmbrack, **symbolising** an impending marriage. But instead the two girls from next door to the Donnelly's have played a trick in one of the Hallowe'en games. Maria is blindfolded and made to feel around for objects and guess what they are. She feels 'a soft wet substance with her fingers' (p. 117), the clay of the title, and it becomes clear that the children have played a joke of which the adults don't approve. The clay might represent death, the return of the body to soil, and so the joke has reminded Maria of her mortality. On her second turn at the game she gets a prayer book, indicating a vocation to a convent life. Either death or the convent suggests sterility.

The story ends with Maria singing a song from an opera called *The Bohemian Girl*. In that song, the young girl, born of noble stock, but having been brought up by gypsies, dreams of her noble roots. This possibly indicates that Maria has a dream to be someone else, to be someone of grander, more important status, and not the diminutive, slight person who is treated almost as if she were dead. Maria makes a mistake in singing the song by repeating the first stanza when she should sing the second stanza.

The omission of the second stanza of the song may indicate the tragedy of Maria's situation. What she neglects to sing is the following:

I dreamt that suitors besought my hand,
That knights upon bended knee,
And with vows no maiden heart could withstand,
That they pledged their faith to me.
And I dreamt that one of this noble host
Came forth my hand to claim;
Yet I also dreamt, which charmed me most,
That you lov'd me still the same.

Maria denies the suggestion of love, then, three times. The first occurs in the institution when Ginger Mooney says she is sure Maria will get the ring, and Maria tells her she wants neither a ring nor a man. The second occurs in the cake shop when the counter-lady asks Maria if she wants a wedding cake, and Maria blushes and smiles, indicating her denial of the suggestion. The third occurs when Maria omits the stanza in which the Bohemian girl sings of her desire for suitors, replacing it with the first stanza about dreaming of greatness and riches. 'Clay' might be seen as the first story in *Dubliners* about the sterility of Dublin life. It is immediately followed by 'A Painful Case' in which a bachelor, Mr Duffy, is similarly incapable of breaking out of his own routine of living alone and loving no-one but himself.

Maria is portrayed in 'Clay' in an ambiguous light. On the one hand, she is shy and reserved, and is treated as a slight, fragile figure by most of the people around her. But on the other hand, the story is told from her point of view, and offers images of her as peace-maker, mother, beautiful, adored friend and generous visitor. It is not clear whether we are reading Maria's illusions about herself, or how other characters see her. Although it is very different in tone and character, the story builds on the images of paralysis and entrapment in the stories preceding it. If Chandler and Farrington in the earlier stories have lashed out in reaction to the narrowness of their own lives (albeit violently and abusively), Maria seems to resign herself almost completely to the limits of her life. In the night on which people celebrate the feast of the waking of the dead on earth, Maria is marked by the sign of death, the clay which surrounds her coffin.

Notice also in this story Joyce's use of repetition, of the synonyms for 'smallness', as mentioned above, but also of the phrase 'Maria laughed again till the tip of her nose nearly met the tip of her chin' (p. 112, cf p. 117). Joyce repeats words and phrases with some frequency as a way of holding a particular image of the character and situation as a constant through the story, and as a way of giving the story a concentrated focus on a precise object.

barmbrack from the Gaelic, bairín breac, meaning speckled cake or bread. A traditional dish at Hallowe'en, barmbracks are a kind of bread containing fruit pieces and currants. They were baked with coins or rings in them, each item **symbolising** a future – riches or marriage, for example

the Board ladies members of the Board of Governors of the Dublin by Lamplight organisation. This Protestant charitable institution gave a home to, and attempted to reform, women who had been prostitutes or alcoholics. Maria works in the scullery in this institution, which makes for an interesting contrast between her primness and the background of the inmates

the dummy a dumb, or mute, person

Ballsbridge a suburb to the south-east of Dublin

the Pillar Nelson's pillar, which once stood on the main street of Dublin, Sackville (now O'Connell) Street (see Maps). The Pillar was erected by the British authorities in memory of Admiral Lord Nelson, 1758–1805

Drumcondra a suburb to the north of Dublin

Whit-Monday a public holiday, the Monday after Pentecost Sunday, seven Sundays after Easter

two half-crowns five shillings

coppers less valuable coins, so called for their copper colour

tracts on the walls Protestant moral and religious sayings or biblical extracts, for the improvement and guidance of the inmates

the ring traditionally baked in the barmbrack as a charm or **symbol**

Hallow Eves Hallowe'en, or All Hallow's Eve, the eve of the feast of All Saints on 1st November every year. Hallowe'en also falls on the Pagan festival of Samhain, the feast of the dead in which the spirits were said to walk the earth, which heralded the beginning of winter

a mass morning the next day, 1st November, is the feast of All Saints, a church feast

apples and nuts traditional snacks at the Hallowe'en feast

Two-and-four two shillings and four pence, an expensive cake

a drop taken euphemism for drunk

Hallow Eve games the games played on this feast night included blindfolding participants and having them choose items from a tray. These items had **symbolic** significance attached: a prayer book meant a vocation to the church, a coin meant riches, a ring for marriage, water meant life or travel

a soft wet substance the girls have placed clay (hence the title) on the saucer as a joke. The clay may **symbolise** death here

Miss McCloud's Reel a traditional Irish tune, played on the fiddle

I Dreamt that I Dwelt a song from Michael William Balfe's opera, *The Bohemian Girl*, also referred to in 'Eveline'. Maria's mistake here is to sing the same stanza, the first stanza, twice

poor old Balfe Balfe had become a very unfashionable composer by this time

A PAINFUL CASE   **Publication: Written in 1905, and revised in 1906. First published in *Dubliners*, 1914.**

James Duffy, the main character in 'A Painful Case', is a man of routine, who lives like a hermit in his room in Chapelizod, to the west of Dublin.

The story begins with a description of the items in his room, which have all been bought by Mr Duffy for his own specific needs, the smells of pencils, gum and over-ripe apple which inhabit the room, and Duffy's curious habits and hobbies which occupy his time at his desk. The room is sparse and well ordered, 'uncarpeted' and 'free from pictures', and reflects Mr Duffy's desire to be self-sufficient. A number of words in the first few lines set up the atmosphere of his environment: 'disused', 'sombre', 'shallow'. Duffy's daily routine is described, including his job as cashier in a bank, his meals and his walks.

His routine is disrupted, however, when he meets a married woman, Mrs Sinico, at a concert, and begins to form a friendship with her. After a few accidental meetings, Mr Duffy and Mrs Sinico arrange to meet each other, sometimes at Mrs Sinico's house. Mrs Sinico's husband is under the misapprehension that Mr Duffy is interested in their daughter, and so therefore pays no attention to the relationship forming between his wife and the gentleman visitor: 'He had dismissed his wife so sincerely from his gallery of pleasures that he did not suspect anyone else would take an interest in her' (p. 122).

Mr Duffy and Mrs Sinico come to depend on their meetings with each other, and the friendship deepens. But whereas Mrs Sinico assumes his expressions of loneliness are cries for love, Mr Duffy is merely pontificating on the necessity of loneliness. Mrs Sinico advances her hand in intimacy to Duffy, but he retreats, repulsed by her failure to understand, and he breaks off the relationship.

Joyce portrays Duffy as a fastidious, hermitic man, frightened of intimacy, and full of absurd principles and notions. The narrative weaves together sympathetic insights into Duffy's mind and feelings with dispassionate observations of his eccentric character. Four years pass, during which Mr Duffy slips back into his orderly, daily routine, until he reads in the evening newspaper one day of the death of Mrs Sinico, having been knocked down on a railway line by a train. The story quotes in full the newspaper account of the incident, including testimonies by Mrs Sinico's daughter and husband to her recent alcoholism and her intemperate habits. Mr Duffy is revolted by the story of the woman that Mrs Sinico had become, and revolted by the thought of his intimacy with her: 'it revolted him to think that he had ever spoken to her of what he held sacred' (p. 128).

He considers her weak and corrupt, but then he begins to think of her loneliness. He realises that in abandoning her, he left her and himself to a life of loneliness. He passes a place in the Phoenix Park where 'some human figures' were having sex, and this causes him further to reflect that he is alone in the world. The description of a goods train pulling out of Kingsbridge railway station, 'like a worm with a fiery head' (p. 131), echoes the fate suffered by Mrs Sinico.

There is much emphasis in this story on the role of narrative. Mr Duffy thinks of the lives of both Mrs Sinico and himself as narratives. The narrative of her death from a newspaper report is quoted at length in the story. His life seems to be measured by the sentences which he writes on his sheets of paper.

Like many of the stories in *Dubliners*, the books and plays which are mentioned indicate some points of significance for the story and the character. In this case, Mr Duffy reads Wordsworth, a poet noted for his musings on solitariness and loneliness, and he reflects on the philosophy of Nietzsche, noted for his thinking on the self-sufficiency, order and ideal discipline of the super-man. He writes, in a pseudo-philosophical style: 'Love between man and man is impossible because there must not be sexual intercourse and friendship between man and woman is impossible because there must be sexual intercourse' (p. 125). Mr Duffy also reads the pro-Unionist Dublin newspaper, not the pro-nationalist newspaper more commonly seen in the hands of ordinary Dubliners. All of these written texts could be seen to identify the character and beliefs of Mr Duffy. He seems, in other words, to reflect what he reads, and to be influenced by what he reads. Much of this emphasis on narrative serves to bring the reader closer to Duffy's own self-image, and the way he wishes others to see him.

There is a further significance to the role of narrative in the story, however. At an early stage of the story, we read of Mr Duffy:

He lived at a little distance from his body, regarding his own acts with doubtful side-glances. He had an odd autobiographical habit which led him to compose in his mind from time to time a short sentence about himself containing a subject in the third person and a predicate in the past tense. (p. 120)

The story is told in relatively short sentences, in the third person and with the predicate in the past tense. Is it possible that the story is itself written by James Duffy, that 'A Painful Case' is Duffy's fiction about himself? Perhaps a fiction constructed around a newspaper report that he has read of a woman he never knew? This might be one approach to the story. Another might be to regard these autobiographical habits of Duffy as part of his absorption in himself, which prevents him from engaging in passion, and traps him in a wearying and painful isolation from the world. Consider the descriptions of his habits and his environment, and the way that these descriptions serve to separate Duffy from the common Dubliners. Like Chandler in 'A Little Cloud', Duffy seems to look down on the people around him, and to avoid contact with them at all costs. He adopts a life of lonely self-sufficiency, a life which is suggestive of a monk's, just as Maria in 'Clay' lives life similar to a convent nun.

From the ways in which Duffy is represented in the story, Joyce seems to regard the whole episode of 'A Painful Case' as a modern tragedy. His lonely life is enlightened and warmed by Mrs Sinico, whose company 'exalted him, wore away the rough edges of his character, emotionalized his mental life' (p. 124). Yet, at the same time, there is something cold and dispassionate in the way that Duffy must always note and ruminate on the effects of every event and conversation on his own character. Duffy seems incapable of genuine feeling and emotion, and Dublin seems to be in part to blame for his painful insularity.

Chapelizod three miles west of the city centre along the river Liffey, and to the south of the Phoenix Park. The name derives from French, 'Chapel d'Iseult', referring to the mythical lovers Tristan and Iseult. Gifford suggests that the Phoenix Park, to which Duffy retreats towards the end of the story, is the Forest of Tristan, to which Tristan goes in despair having realised the impossibility of his love for Iseult (see Further Reading)

a complete Wordsworth a book of the complete poetry of William Wordsworth, English Romantic poet, 1770–1850, indicating at this time Duffy's rather conservative tastes

the Maynooth Catechism Maynooth is the Irish centre for the education of

Catholic priests, and the Maynooth Catechism was the definitive guide to the principles of Irish Catholic belief

Hauptmann's Michael Kramer a four-act play by German playwright and novelist, Gerhart Hauptmann. Michael Kramer is an isolated and single-minded man, like Duffy, who struggles against the philistinism and corruption he sees all around him

Bile Beans a popular cure for bilious conditions

saturnine born under the influence of the watery planet, Saturn, and therefore a heavy, dull and melancholic character

a stout hazel a walking stick made of hazel wood

Dan Burke's a public house on Baggot Street lower, to the east of St Stephen's Green (see Maps)

Mozart's music Wolfgang Amadeus Mozart, 1756–91, Austrian musical genius and composer

Leghorn an Italian port, Livorno

Irish Socialist Party some small socialist parties and groups had been established by this time, including James Connolly's Irish Socialist Republican Party, founded in 1896, but mostly Irish politics were more concerned with rural land issues than with the plight of labour during this period

Nietzsche Friedrich Nietzsche, 1844–1900, German philosopher, wrote of the coming of the over- or super-man, who would reject the herd-animal morality of the masses and would help humanity towards civilisation by living a reclusive life, dedicated to discipline and order. The appeal for Duffy is obvious. The subsequent musings on love and friendship are borrowed from Nietzsche too

Mail the *Dublin Evening Mail*, printed on buff-coloured paper, a right-wing, pro-Unionist paper

Secreto Latin for secret or set apart, and referring to the part of Catholic mass when the priest whispers the words of a prayer over the Eucharist offerings

Sydney Parade Station railway station located in the south-east suburbs of Dublin

a league a temperance or abstinence league, which would help Mrs Sinico to give up her drinking habits

Herald the *Evening Herald*, a Dublin newspaper of nationalist sympathies

IVY DAY IN THE COMMITTEE ROOM

Publication: Written in 1905. First published in *Dubliners*, 1914.

'Ivy Day in the Committee Room' does not tell a story so much as represent a conversation between Dubliners who are engaged in organising and canvassing for an election for the city council. The characters represent a wide range of political opinions, from Hynes the nationalist to Crofton the conservative.

The first topic of their conversation is parenting, but when the nationalist Hynes enters the conversation turns to politics. Socialism is briefly discussed as Hynes stands up for the working man, and displays his republican ideals in mocking the English monarchy: 'What do we want kowtowing to a foreign king?' (p. 136). The conversation is interspersed with references to the municipal elections in which they are all involved. It becomes clear that many of the men present have lost interest in politics in the aftermath of Parnell's death.

There is a general atmosphere of apathy pervading their discussion. This begins when O'Connor lights a cigarette using the election card of the candidate he is canvassing for, Richard Tierney, indicating his indifference to the election. Old Jack and O'Connor then express the sentiment that times were better, and politics more vibrant, when Parnell was alive. Many of the men are wearing the ivy symbol denoting their mark of respect for the anniversary of Parnell's death. This theme of a political scene which has turned stagnant and dull becomes the subject of the remainder of their discussion. The discussion reflects the view that the death of Parnell left a political void in Ireland. No-one seems to have even the enthusiasm to maintain their own convictions.

Lyons and Crofton, both of whom are known supporters of union-ism, canvass for a nationalist candidate, and the nationalist men are gathered around the fire in the Committee Room because they have not even the enthusiasm for their own candidate to bear the rain. Nothing is the same since Parnell's death. The priest, Father McKeon, is far from certain of his convictions, and when he first enters it cannot be discerned whether he was 'a poor clergyman or a poor actor' (p. 140). The mayor is believed to be less than satisfactory too, with tales of how he lives like a poor man. The story ends with Hynes reciting his poem in honour of Parnell, and with the conservative Crofton commenting that the poem 'was a very fine piece of writing' (p. 152). His polite response indicates that, although he is not a nationalist, even he acknowledges Parnell as an important figure, and that his belief in conservatism is not strong enough to incite him to counter the ideas represented in the poem.

> The stagnancy of Irish politics, as represented in this story, is another dimension of the paralysis of Dublin life. At no point in the story do we learn anything of Richard Tierney's views or proposals, only that he is a moderate nationalist. The men canvassing for Tierney are far more interested in their pay, in drinking (the sound of corks popping – 'pok!' – interrupts the conversation at several points) and in lamenting the passing of the old times, in which Parnell gave Irish nationalism its voice in the British parliament in London.

> The men represent very different political viewpoints and yet all seem to be consenting to canvass for the one nationalist candidate. Although this indicates some kind of consensus, it is a consensus bred out of indifference and apathy, not of conviction. Everyone seems to lack conviction in *Dubliners*. Just as Mr Duffy believes that there will be no social revolution in Ireland because the workers are too interested in the quick pay rise rather than achieving socialist ideals, the men in the Committee Room cannot get excited about the municipal elections because nothing will change.

> The language used by the men is non-committal and mild: 'I think he'll be all right' (p. 137), 'he's not so bad', 'it's better than nothing', 'He's not a bad sort' (all p. 144), and the final line of the story, spoken by Mr Crofton about the poem on Parnell, 'it was a very fine piece of writing' (p. 152). Hynes at the end of the story does not hear the invitation to drink because he is locked into his memories of Parnell, conjured up by the poem. We might also consider the extent to which the story is mocking these men, not just for their apathy, but for their duplicity. They are fighting for a nationalist candidate, and yet they talk of forgiving and welcoming the English king, who the moderate nationalist, Henchy, describes as 'a good sportsman' (p. 148).

Ivy Day in the Committee Room Ivy Day, 6th October, was the day on which the Irish home rule leader, Charles Stewart Parnell, 1846–91, was commemorated by Irish nationalists every year after his death. Nationalists wore a leaf of dark green ivy to symbolise the rebirth of home rule ideals. Parnell had led the attempts to win a limited form of legislative independence for Ireland from the British Parliament. He was involved in a relationship with a married woman, Kitty O'Shea, which brought him into disrepute, particularly strong criticism coming from the Catholic church. As a result he was deposed from leadership of the home rule party in Committee Room 15 of the Houses of Parliament in London in December 1890. He died on 6th October 1891, and there followed a cult worship of Parnell in moderate nationalist circles in Ireland, where he was renowned as 'the uncrowned king of Ireland', and was often referred to simply as 'the chief'

Municipal Elections elections to the governing body of the Dublin Corporation. About one in nine of Dublin's citizens were entitled to vote

Royal Exchange Ward in the centre of the city on the south-side of the Liffey

P.L.G. Poor Law Guardian, elected by local ratepayers to oversee the distribution of the scarce relief funds of the parish to the poor and needy, and to supervise schemes of work for the unemployed. Usually regarded as oppressive taskmasters over the poor

Wicklow Street south of the Liffey, and home to the area headquarters of the nationalist party, hence the location of the Committee Room in which the story is set

the Christian Brothers a teaching order founded in 1802, running schools for lower class boys, emphasising trade and practical skills

cocks him up slang for cheers him up, or boosts his ego

a sup taken slang for drunk

bowsy slang for ruffian

a Freemason's meeting a joke that the meeting of the men is of the secret society of businessmen and traders, often associated in Ireland with Unionism and pro-British attitudes

tinker traveller or gypsy

shoneens from the Irish for little John Bull, meaning an Irish person who attempts to succeed by mimicking English ways and manners

a handle to his name a title to his name. In this context, meaning bowing to the aristocracy

hunker-sliding to slide while sitting on one's heels, and so not to slide 'straight', hence to act with duplicity, or to be dishonest

a German monarch Edward VII, king of the United Kingdom, descended from German aristocracy

Edward Rex Edward VII, who was expected to pay a royal visit to Ireland in early 1903, only a few months after the time in which the story was set

the Nationalist ticket standing as a candidate for the Irish Nationalist Party, advocating home rule for Ireland

spondulics slang for money

Musha also 'usha, from the Irish 'muise', meaning 'well!', or 'indeed!'

hand-me-down shop a shop selling second-hand clothes

the houses public houses

moya! an exclamation used ironically to mean 'as if', or 'as it were'

a decent skin slang for a decent person

hillsiders and fenians rebels and nationalists

the Castle Dublin Castle was the centre of British administrative and police authority in Ireland, including police intelligence services, responsible for gathering information on rebels from informants

Major Sirr Sirr was British mayor of Dublin during the 1798 rebellion, during which he was responsible for the brutal methods used to crush rebellion and to arrest rebel leaders

the Black Eagle a fictional pub

very thick in this context, the two men were thick means that they were great friends

Kavanagh's a pub near Dublin Castle, renowned as a gathering place for politicians and lobbyists

a black sheep meaning that Father Keon doesn't conform to what is expected of him, or doesn't adhere to the conventions of the priesthood

how does he knock it out how does he make a living?

goster gossip

Yerra from the Irish 'aire', meaning 'look you'

hop-o'-my-thumb small person

Mansion House official residence of the mayor of Dublin

my vermin the mayor wears ceremonious robes which are ermine-trimmed. Henchy is either dropping a **malapropism** here, or he is satirising the mayor by suggesting an association with vermin

tinpot way small, or inferior way

thin edge of the wedge euphemism for a start

Did the cow calve? did you have good luck?

the Conservatives the Irish Conservative Party, a Unionist party aligned with the British Conservative Party, and differing on very few issues

Didn't Parnell himself ... Parnell had asked nationalists in 1885 to avoid all celebrations of the visit of Edward VII, then prince, to Ireland, but he also counselled Irish people against showing any sign of disrespect or protest so as to maintain his diplomatic efforts to secure home rule in the London parliament

his old mother Joyce initially had written 'his bloody ould mother' here, but was forced to drop the word 'bloody' to get published. The phrase refers to Queen Victoria, who had reigned in Britain from 1837 to 1901, a long period of reign

The old one never went to see these wild Irish in the English colonial stereotypes of the Irish, wildness and savagery were used frequently. It is not true that Victoria never visited Ireland. She had visited Ireland as recently as 1900 when she was welcomed enthusiastically in Dublin. The error on Henchy's part (or maybe Joyce's) seems unusual

A MOTHER   Publication: Written in 1905. First published in *Dubliners*, 1914.

'A Mother' is about the arrangement between Mrs Kearney and Mr Holohan to have her daughter play the piano in accompaniment at Mr Holohan's concerts. Mrs Kearney, née Devlin, is from a bourgeois background in which she has acquired talents and accomplishments which ought to earn her a suitable marriage partner.

The language of the story at this point indicates the crude ambitions and materialist interests of the bourgeois (for example, 'She sat amid the chilly circle of her accomplishments, waiting for some suitor to brave it and offer her a brilliant life' p. 153). Although she is renowned for her manners and for her musical ability, she does not attract a sufficiently brilliant suitor, and, under pressure from her friends and her age, she marries a dull, pious but respectable gentleman bootmaker. From this point on, the story conveys the impression that Mrs Kearney and her husband are living vicariously through their daughter. He is putting money aside for her dowry, and she is 'determined to take advantage of her daughter's name' (p. 154) to put her through Irish lessons and music lessons.

When Mr Holohan arrives to ask Mrs Kearney's daughter to play at his four concerts, it is Mrs Kearney who does all the negotiating, and insists on a contract for eight guineas. Mrs Kearney is intent on earning status and money for her daughter (and herself). The concerts prove to be unsuccessful, with the first two nights badly attended by people of the wrong class for Mrs Kearney. The third night is cancelled. All effort goes into the fourth night, which is well attended, and of reasonable quality. Asserting herself, Mrs Kearney insists on the money being paid to her daughter before the concert, and when Mr Holohan and Mr Fitzpatrick, the concert organisers, put up resistance, Mrs Kearney threatens not to allow her daughter to play.

Mrs Kearney's ego is evidently her own main concern: 'They thought they had only a girl to deal with' (p. 166). She gets less than half the money before Mr Holohan loses his patience with her threats. Miss Healy, a friend of the Kearneys, takes Kathleen Kearney's place as piano accompanist, and the Kearneys leave, with the concert organisers convinced that Kathleen Kearney will never work in Dublin's music circles again.

> Another form of paralysis is exhibited in this story. Mrs Kearney is trapped into a dull marriage and an unrewarding life, in contrast to the brilliant life she expected as a young woman. As a result, she lives out her lost hopes and dreams through her daughter, who in turn is trapped by the tyranny of her mother's hopes. But the trap is wider, for in this story the whole of Dublin's artistic and musical community is seen to thrive on second-rate acts, retired music hall singers from London, and tired and nervous tenors afraid of the audience. Concerts are arranged ad hoc, and Dublin's musical community appears provincial and stale.
>
> The attitude of the bourgeois class to art and music is satirised in this story. Certainly, Mrs Kearney treated her musical endeavours as the means to find a suitable (affluent) partner, and the intention behind Mrs Kearney's manipulations of her daughter's musical abilities is also social climbing. Art and music are used by the middle classes as means to materialist ends, ways of meeting richer, more respectable people. The story is a satire on the interests of this class in Irish nationalism and the Irish revival too.

The extent of the Kearney's nationalism is that Kathleen sends Irish picture postcards to her friends, and that Mrs Kearney uses the Irish Revival movements for the purposes of social climbing. This is evident in the emphasis on social networking at the beginning of the story, with the Kearneys meeting 'their friends' outside the Cathedral, and playing 'every little counter of gossip', and in the concern for what is 'on people's lips' (pp. 154–5). The Dublin middle classes are presented here as shallow, narrow-minded, without any real feeling for any form of culture or belief, and trapped in a provincial, materialist mentality.

Eire Abu Ireland for Victory, showing that the Society is part of the Irish nationalist revival

every first Friday a Catholic practice of attending the Eucharist on the first Friday of every month. Jesus Christ was supposed to have told St Margaret Mary Alacoque that a believer who practised this devotion would be sure to receive the sacraments and blessings before death

a society a friendly society, or building society, which provided savings policies for weddings, trusts, funerals, and so on

the Academy the Royal Academy of Music, on Merrion Square (see Maps)

Skerries … Howth … Greystones fishing villages on the coast near Dublin which were popular summer resorts for Dubliners

the Irish Revival in the 1890s there was a major surge of interest in Irish language, literature, culture and sports. The Irish language had almost disappeared as a native language by this time, and the Irish language movement played a key role in reviving interest in all aspects of Irish culture, including music and dance

her daughter's name Kathleen, a name associated with Ireland through the legend of Kathleen Ni Houlihan, or the Countess Cathleen, the poor old woman of Ireland, made prominent during this period by W.B. Yeats

the pro-cathedral the church used by Catholics as a cathedral, since the two Dublin cathedrals belonged to the Protestant Church of Ireland

Antient Concert Rooms in Brunswick Street Great, now Pearse Street, a venue for concerts and meetings

charmeuse trimming for a garment

Brown Thomas drapers and merchants of silk, lace and linens, located in Grafton Street

Cometty Mrs Kearney is imitating Fitzpatrick's flat accent

the General Post Office the centre of postal communications in Dublin and Ireland, and an impressive architectural landmark, with classical facade, located in the main thoroughfare of the city centre, Sackville Street, now O'Connell Street

Maritana popular light opera by Irish composer, William Vincent Wallace, 1812–65

the Queen's Theatre one of the three major theatres in Dublin at this time, it hosted a mixture of musicals, operas and dramas

yous adds 's' to the plural for 'you', a common **colloquialism**

Feis Ceoil annual music festival and competition, started in 1897, with the aim of promoting interest and quality in Irish music and culture. James Joyce is said to have been awarded a bronze medal in this contest in 1904

the *Freeman* man the journalist or reviewer from the *Freeman's Journal*, a Dublin newspaper

Mrs Pat Campbell an important English actress of the time, 1865–1940, and a friend of George Bernard Shaw

Killarney a popular sentimental song from *Innisfallen*, by Michael William Balfe, 1808–1870. See 'Eveline'

fol-the-diddle-I-do a phrase meaning 'what do I care?', or implying generally an attitude of carelessness or being carefree

GRACE   Publication: Written in 1905. First published in *Dubliners*, 1914.

'Grace' is the story of Mr Kernan, who is found lying unconscious in the underground lavatory of a public house, and who is gradually persuaded by friends and acquaintances to take up religion rather than drink. Kernan is a commercial traveller who could be said to have 'fallen from grace', and therefore the title of the story gives us the ideal that Kernan must reach, the return to 'grace'.

The story is divided into three parts. Firstly, the discovery of Kernan lying unconscious, and his being unknown until Mr Power, an old friend recognises him. Secondly, Kernan's convalescence in his home, with a group of his friends gathered around him plotting to get him to join them on a religious retreat. Thirdly, then, Kernan's attendance at the church with his friends, and the priest's discussion of his role as the 'spiritual accountant' of these businessmen and professional people (p. 198). The ending of the story is ambiguous about whether Kernan is redeemed, because it is the priest's voice which is allowed to end the story. The narrative concerning Kernan is, in effect, over. He has ceased to be the focus of the story, and attention is now given to the priest's sermon to the congregation on how they are to be redeemed.

A closer look at how the story works may help us to identify its religious significance. The story begins with a scene of squalor. Kernan is depicted as a fallen man, 'smeared with the filth and ooze of the floor' (p. 169), and his speech when he regains consciousness seems slurred and deformed. In religious terms, the fall from grace is then the fall of Man. Kernan represents the descent of man into sin. We begin in hell, the underground lavatory of sin and filth. A selfless angel, aptly named Mr Power, rescues Kernan from this place where he is unknown and uncared for. He takes Kernan to his home, where his family suffer for his sins, and Kernan lies in his sickbed, the purgatory in which he must be converted to a good man before he can, as the priest says, be received into everlasting dwellings. In the quotation that the priest gives the motives for the plot to redeem Kernan may be found:

For the children of this world are wiser in their generation than the children of light.
Wherefore make unto yourselves friends out of the mammon of iniquity so that when you die
they may receive you into everlasting dwellings (p. 197)

Kernan's friends rescue him from iniquity and bring him through purgatory to heaven. In one interpretation of this story, the church represents heaven, and the reason why Kernan disappears from the narrative at the end is that he becomes one of the 'great congregation in the sky'. He has passed into the unity of souls in heaven, and is worshipping the word of God with his congregation. But the revelation of Kernan's redemption, his ascension into heaven, is based on the absence of Kernan. The **epiphany** or revelation of this story is based on **ellipsis** (see Epiphany in Techniques). **Ellipsis** means a piece of information or text which is omitted or absent. The ellipsis of Kernan allows the story to present a chip of reality that has **symbolic** force. And it has **symbolic** force by virtue of its being able to imagine the journey from man's fall to his ascension into the kingdom of heaven. In this sense it is reminiscent of Dante's *Divine Comedy*. But it is also **symbolic** of other facets of Catholic theology.

Irish Catholicism becomes the focus of the story in the way that theological issues are represented through the scenes and characters. In the middle of the story a discussion of papal infallibility takes place. In this scene, Joyce constructs the idea of Catholicism from the point of view of the Dublin middle classes, allowing their banter about the Jesuits, the Pope, mottoes and ceremonies, and the high drama of theological debates within the Vatican to make a farce of the situation. The seriousness and respectful attention in which this talk, often erroneous, of papal infallibility takes place elevates the sense of **irony** that is being developed.

The crucial element in making sense of Joyce's story here is the point of view from which the story is being told. For example, papal infallibility is made palatable to the society of businessmen by appealing to their sense of nationalism, by showing them that it was an Irishman, John MacHale, who resisted, and then submitted to, the authority of the Pope. The ending of the story, bearing in mind this pious middle class from whose point of view the story is being told, represents the just reward of the four 'evangelists', as Frank O'Connor called them: Cunningham, Power, M'Coy and Fogarty.

This version of the ending would place an **ironic** twist on the idea of spiritual accountancy, a balancing of the spiritual books, and would make 'Grace' a deeply satirical look at the pious religious attitudes as well as the mean minded self-interest of the professional and business classes, whose spirituality can only be reached through an appeal to accountancy and nationalism. Even religion becomes a business to them, an opportunity for profit (albeit spiritual profit).

Grace grace in the Catholic faith is the state of virtue given to us by God. It also refers to the period of time which a debtor has to make good his debt. The story begins after Kernan has fallen, hence the suggestion that he has fallen from grace

curates barmen of junior status

Sha' derived from Irish for 'yes', or 'it is'

an outsider a two-wheeled cart with seats perpendicular to the axle, therefore giving the sense of riding on the outside of the cart

the great Blackwhite not known for certain, but appears to have been a legendary salesman

E.C. the postal district of the commercial centre of London, now subdivided into EC1, EC2, EC3 and EC4

Royal Irish Constabulary the R.I.C. was an armed para-military police force under the direction of the Lord Lieutenant, and responsible for the suppression of rebellion and dissidence in Ireland. The headquarters of the R.I.C. was Dublin Castle, on the south-side of the city (see Maps)

what book they were in different books were used on the curricula for each school year, and so Power is asking the children what school year they are in

Fogarty's a tea, wine and spirits merchant off the North Circular Road, on the northern rim of Dublin

Sandymount suburban seaside village to the south-east of Dublin

the pale in early colonial Ireland, in the fourteenth and fifteenth centuries, the pale was the area around Dublin and to the north of it controlled by English forces. To go beyond the pale, according to English representations, was to go into wild, savage, unknown territory, the home of the 'wild Irish'. To be in the pale meant to be safe, protected, and under some kind of secure, civilised authority

Sacred Heart a popular image or icon of the heart of Jesus Christ

banshee a popular Irish legend of the spirit of an old woman who wails and chants on the eve of a death in the house

Midland Railway the Great Western and Midland Railway which served Galway, Athlone, Mullingar, and many other places in mid- and western Ireland

the sub-sheriff responsible for evictions, confiscations and repossessions

the Liffey Loan Bank fictional, but similar organisations were abundant in Dublin at the time, which would lend money to the poor at exorbitant interest rates

peloothered drunk

True bill Kernan is using a phrase employed by a grand jury to confirm that there is sufficient evidence of guilt for the accused to be put to trial

bostoons from the Irish for a soft rod made from rushes, referring pejoratively to a spineless, spiritless person

omadhauns from the Irish for fools or idiots

yahoos depraved beasts, or hooligans, contrasted with the wise, rational horses in Jonathan Swift's *Gulliver's Travels* (1726)

M'Auley's a pub close to the place of retreat

to make a retreat to go to a place, usually church property, for a period of spiritual and religious reflection

the General of the Jesuits the Jesuit order is one of the most renowned in the Catholic Church, respected for its successes in missionary and in educational work. The order is led by a General, who is elected for life and answers directly to the Pope. Gifford notes that the order was once suppressed and re-organised in the late eighteenth century, contradicting Cunningham's claim that the Jesuits were never reformed (see Further Reading)

secular priests secular priests live in parishes and are appointed to the parish. This contrasts with religious orders like the Jesuits, who live in monasteries or houses, and have less worldly tasks to perform

back of the ... pit Kernan stumbles upon the word 'pit', which is a theatrical term, displaying his ignorance of the church. He is referring to the nave of the church

The Prisoner of the Vatican King Victor Emmanuel II defeated the papal army in 1860 in the wars which led to the creation of a united Italy in 1861. He captured Rome from the Pope, and since then the church has been confined to the Vatican city, hence Pope Pius IX was known as 'prisoner of the Vatican' (as were his successors)

Orangeman a Unionist, or member of the Protestant Orange Order

Pope Leo XIII also a prisoner of the Vatican, pope from 1878 to 1903, the successor to Pius IX

Lux upon Lux this, and 'Crux upon Crux', are absurd because they combine Latin and English, and because popes did not choose mottoes, or have mottoes attached to them

penny-a-week school schools for the poor run by a private teacher who charged fees at a penny a week

with a sod of turf under his oxter the turf was his contribution to the fuel supply as payment for schooling. Oxter is slang for armpit

Great minds are very near to madness a misquotation of Dryden's 'Great wits are sure to madness near allied', from *Absalom and Achitophel* (1681)

up to the knocker up to standard

ex cathedra meaning literally from the chair of his office, but when the Pope speaks ex cathedra he is infallible

John MacHale archbishop of Tuam in Ireland, 1835–76. A rebel archbishop who convinced the Vatican to sever diplomatic links with Britain in 1850, and who opposed papal infallibility until it was adopted by the Vatican Council of 1870. As Brown notes in the Penguin Twentieth-Century Classics edition of *Dubliners*, neither Dollinger nor MacHale were at the Vatican Council, so the story of their famous resistance and submission is entirely fictitious

Sir John Gray a Protestant Irish nationalist, 1815–75, councillor, member of parliament, and owner and editor of the *Freeman's Journal*. MacHale did attend the unveiling ceremony for Gray's statue, which stands in O'Connell Street

Edmund Dwyer Gray son of the above, and also a nationalist, although more moderate. He also owned and edited the *Freeman's Journal*

baptismal vows the vows at a Catholic baptism ceremony are taken by the godparents of the child in her or his name. The vows consist mostly of renouncing the devil, and being a faithful and devout believer. Occasionally adults renew these vows to God

I bar the candles one of the major differences between Catholic and Protestant ceremonies is that Catholic ceremonies tend to use candles, images and icons both to adorn the church and as **symbols** of Catholic faith. Protestant reformers saw many of these objects as redundant decorations which were attempts to dazzle and mystify, hence Kernan's reference to 'magic-lantern business' (p. 194)

lay-brother some religious orders include lay-members, who have not become priests and who can perform minor daily chores

speck of red light a red light above the sanctuary indicates the presence of the blessed sacraments of wine/blood and bread/body

quincunx a set of five points – four at corners and one in the centre – **symbolising** the wounds of Christ at the crucifixion

For the children of this world ... from the Gospel according to Luke, 16:8–9. The parable involves a businessman who is accused of waste, for which Jesus asks him to account

Mammon a pagan god representing wealth

THE DEAD   Publication: Written in 1907. First published in *Dubliners*, 1914.

The longest story in the *Dubliners* collection, 'The Dead' is the story of Gabriel Conroy who attends the Christmas dinner party of his aunts, the

Morkans, accompanied by his wife Gretta. The story begins with the arrival of the Conroys at the house of the Misses Morkans, where they are greeted by the maid, Lily.

The Morkans are middle class ladies who have been prominent in Dublin music circles, and who host entertaining evenings for their friends and family. Gabriel is a self-conscious, intellectual character, often embarrassed and sometimes snobbish. He is embarrassed by Lily who tells him, 'the men that is now is only all palaver' (p. 202), a premonition of the conclusion in which Gabriel realises that he is a shadow of the man who died for his wife. He is embarrassed also by Miss Ivors, who teases him for having written reviews in a pro-British newspaper, and for not supporting the revival movement in his own country. She accuses him of being a British sympathiser, a West Briton, and taunts him about not visiting the west of Ireland, 'your own land' (p. 215), then reputed as the last refuge of ancient Gaelic culture.

Joyce sets up an **antithesis** between pro-British and pro-Irish in Gabriel's meeting with Miss Ivors, between West Briton and West of Ireland. This is significant in the conclusion, when Gabriel's imagination travels to the west of Ireland. At the dinner party, we gain an insight into how Conroy acts in public, his quiet reliability, his public persona. He is respected and trusted, and he is also respectful, although we do see his private thoughts here revealing that he doesn't really care for his two aunts, who are referred to as 'two ignorant old women' (p. 219).

Outside the party, we see his passions rising, his contemplation of life with Gretta, and the swell of his frustrations and his sense of excitement. This prepares us for the final tragic scene in which it is revealed to Gabriel that he is not the ideal love of Gretta's life, and he becomes aware of himself as a pathetic shadow of what he should be. In Gretta's comparison of him to Michael Furey, Gabriel sees himself as a shade of that which he imagines himself. Against the burning truth of Furey's death, the discovery that Furey's love must be stronger in her heart than his life as a husband to her, Gabriel is moved to tears, and moved to change his life.

The Dead – dead lovers, dead memories – serve to remind him of who he really is. They come back to haunt him, and the final image of snow falling across every part of Ireland, on all the gravestones and all the universe, creates the **symbolic** atmosphere of the story, in which Gabriel's decision to go westwards signals a change in Ireland, a consciousness of the dead, 'the full glory of some passion' (p. 255) in the other world. This self-realisation is the final **epiphanic** moment of the story, where the main character, and the whole trend of the story, come upon a dramatic revelation.

The religious and political symbols in this story are particularly significant. Note that the story contains the two most powerful angels in Christian mythology – Gabriel (Conroy) and Michael (Furey). Gabriel is depicted as lofty, benevolent, the reliable assistant and admirer of his aunts, and the self-conscious intellectual. If his name indicates his own image of himself, the story also shows us the downfall of the angel, his realisation that he is smaller and less powerful than he thinks. Gabriel falls to earth when he sees his shadow in the mirror, 'a ludicrous figure, acting as a pennyboy for his aunts, a nervous well-meaning sentimentalist', a 'pitiable fatuous fellow' (p. 251), and when he sees himself compared to Michael, who has braved death for the love of Gretta. Death, particularly a heroic or **symbolic** death, as Michael Furey's death is suggested to have been, reminds Gabriel of his insignificance, his lack of power.

The two resemble the reputations of the arch-angels, in that Gabriel is reputed for heralding the birth of John the Baptist and Jesus, while Michael has the more 'heroic' reputation of battling against Satan. In the story, Michael is associated with nationalist struggle through the song, *The Lass of Aughrim*, a nationalist ballad, and therefore with a heroic death. Gabriel in contrast merely heralds the passing of the old generation, and the arrival of a new generation, while his own part, even in his own wife's affections, is somehow minute and unheroic. It is possible also to interpret this story as a passage through the hell of the Morkan's household, to the purgatory of the coach ride, to the final vision of moving across white fields towards paradise in the conclusion.

Joyce uses the **antithesis** of the West of Ireland against the West Briton, in order to create the tension that we see in Gabriel Conroy. The West of Ireland within the story comes to **symbolise** Irish nationalism, a force that Conroy never directly refers to, but for which he implies his dislike, suggesting by his speech that nationalism goes against the traditions of Irish hospitality. Miss Ivors manages to provoke and make fun of Gabriel Conroy by setting him up as the **antithesis** of everything Irish. They seem to represent two different attitudes to Ireland: one cultured and elite which sees nothing of cultural value in Ireland and celebrates European and British traditions, the other ambitious and educated, turning inwards towards Irish traditions to find a haven of native culture.

This same **antithesis** between West Irish and West British is represented in that dramatic end to the story where Gabriel Conroy's remote and cerebral self-consciousness is contrasted with Michael Furey, the young boy who died for Gretta Conroy, who represents not only love, passion and instinct, but also **symbolises** Irish nationalism. Gabriel Conroy resolves this **antithesis** by choosing one side, and we see this choice at the end of the story:

The time had come for him to set out on his journey westward. Yes, the newspapers were right: snow was general all over Ireland. It was falling on every part of the dark central plain, on the treeless hills, falling softly upon the Bog of Allen and, farther westward, softly falling into the dark mutinous Shannon waves. It was falling, too, upon every part of the lonely churchyard on the hill where Michael Furey lay buried. (pp. 255–6)

As a conclusion to the collection, this passage suggests the possibility of a turn to the West of Ireland as a source of inspiration to break out of the paralysis of the city, and it also suggests a shift outwards to the provinces which Joyce intended to be the subject of a further volume of stories.

the Academy the Royal Irish Academy of Music
Antient Concert Rooms in Brunswick Street Great, south-side. Concert halls, also mentioned in 'A Mother'
Adam and Eve's popular name for St Francis of Assisi church, east of Usher's Island
screwed drunk
goloshes overshoes made of India rubber
three syllables Lily pronounces Gabriel's surname as Con-er-oy, indicating her flat Dublin accent

Robert Browning English poet, 1812–89, certainly regarded as a difficult poet in the early twentieth century

the Melodies the accessible and popular melodies of Thomas Moore, which Gabriel thinks would be more to the taste of his companions

Port and Docks Dublin Port and Docks Board, which managed the port facilities

Monkstown affluent village to the south of Dublin (see Maps)

Merrion a village south-east of Dublin, on the bay

dumb-bells weights used for physical exercises

Christy Minstrels the group which made minstrel shows popular, with their imitations of southern negro songs and their blackened face actors, first performing in 1840s New York. Gifford notes that the name had become synonymous with all minstrel shows (see Further Reading)

the Gresham expensive hotel on Sackville (now O'Connell) Street

Quadrilles a square dance

the pledge a Catholic oath to abstain from drinking alcohol

Academy piece the musical piece which would show off her ability and competence to the Royal Irish Academy of Music

Romeo and Juliet the famous balcony scene from Shakespeare, Act 2, Scene 1, with Juliet on the balcony and Romeo below

two murdered princes in the Tower Richard III, king of England 1483–85, was said to have had his two nephew princes killed in the Tower of London in order to protect his claim to the throne

tabinet watered fabric of silk and wool

Balbriggan town about twenty miles north of Dublin, on the coast of the Irish Sea

the Royal University examining and degree-awarding institution which set the curricula of member institutions. Replaced by the National University of Ireland

Lancers a kind of square dance

an Irish device indicating the popular revival of Irish and Celtic designs in jewellery, dress and other objects in the 1890s

The Daily Express a Dublin unionist, pro-British newspaper

West Briton slang for Irish person who sympathises with British rule, and therefore treats Ireland as a province west of Britain

the University question Trinity College, Dublin, retained the reputation of a Protestant university, which troubled the Catholic hierarchy. Some attempts were made to found a Catholic University in Dublin to serve the Catholic population, but in the early twentieth century University College, Dublin, the Catholic university, was still without proper degree-awarding powers

the Aran Isles islands off the west coast of Ireland, near Galway, inhabited by Gaelic-speaking communities. At the turn of the century, they were considered to be the last bastion of Gaelic culture by Irish revivalists

Kathleen Kearney the character from 'A Mother'

visiting together part of the dance, in which the two become dancing partners

the park Phoenix Park, in the west of the city

Wellington Monument obelisk erected in 1817 in commemoration of the British military commander, Arthur Wellesley, Duke of Wellington, 1769–1852

the Three Graces from Greek mythology: Agalaia (Brilliance), Euphrosyne (Joy) and Thalia (Bloom)

Paris from Greek mythology: son of Priam, king of Troy, who was called to judge the contest between the three goddesses of Olympus. Afterwards, Paris ran away with Helen, wife of King Menelaus, thus starting the Trojan War

Arrayed for the Bridal a song from Vincenzo Bellini's opera, *I Puritani* (The Puritans), 1835

the pope to turn out the women out of the choirs in 1903 Pope Pius X decreed that women could not perform the offices of singers in church choirs, and that female parts (sopranos, contraltos) were to be sung by boys

the other persuasion in this case, a euphemism for protestant

a pick itself colloquial saying for 'have a bite'

Beannacht libh Gaelic for farewell

the Theatre Royal one of three principal theatres in Dublin at this time, located just south of the Liffey in Hawkins Street

Gaiety another of Dublin's principal theatres, on South King Street, off St Stephen's Green

Mignon French opera by Ambroise Thomas, 1886

Tietjens ... Aramburo a list of popular opera singers of the nineteenth century

the old Royal Theatre Royal, burned down in 1880, replaced by New Theatre Royal

Let me like a soldier fall song from the opera *Maritana*, by William Vincent Wallace, in which the hero pleads for an honourable death by firing squad

Dinorah Giacomo Meyerbeer's opera, also known as *Le Pardon de Ploermel*, 1859

Lucrezia Borgia Gaetano Donizetti's opera, 1833

Caruso famous tenor, Enrico Caruso, 1873–1921

Mount Melleray Cistercian monastery in Waterford, in the south-east of Ireland. The monks gave hospitality freely to visitors, and the monastery was also known as a refuge for reforming alcoholics

slept in their coffins a misconception – the monks sleep in their habits, and they are also buried in their habits

Fifteen Acres large open field in the Phoenix Park, on which there were military manoeuvres and drills

like the gas meaning on permanent supply, like piped gas

King Billy's Statue a statue of King William III of England (who ruled from 1689 to 1702). He defeated Catholic King James II at the Battle of the Boyne 1690, and re-conquered Ireland. Many Irish units fought against William in what amounted to an attempt to liberate Ireland from Protestant English rule. The statue stood outside Trinity College, Dublin, and was frequently defaced and daubed with mocking slogans

old Irish tonality Gifford notes that early Irish music had a five-tone scale, difficult to translate into more modern scales (see Further Reading)

The Lass of Aughrim Irish song about a peasant girl seduced by a lord, who leaves her with child. The girl seeks out the lord, only to be turned away by his mother, who pretends to be the lord. The girl and her child are drowned when they put to sea, and the lord, who has dreamt of the girl's visit, arrives to see them drowned. The song became renowned as a nationalist ballad, with the lass of Aughrim, in the west of Ireland, **symbolic** of Ireland and the lord of English aristocracy

the Four Courts on the north bank of the Liffey, the seat of the highest courts of Ireland

O'Connell Bridge the bridge leading on to Sackville (now O'Connell) Street, named after Daniel O'Connell, the reformer who pressed for Catholic Emancipation and the Repeal of the Union

the statue of Daniel O'Connell, facing the bridge

sovereign gold sovereign, one pound

go out walking with **colloquial** saying for dating or courting

great with him intimate, or affectionate with. Can refer to friends as well as lovers

Oughterard small village in the west of Ireland in county Galway

Nun's Island a street on the island of that name in Galway city, so called because of the convent located on the island. Galway is built on the island formed by the Galway river

Bog of Allen west of Dublin, a large bog

Shannon the Shannon river which runs from the north-west to the south-west of Ireland, stretching 144 miles and defining much of the border of the western province of Ireland, Connaught

PART THREE

CRITICAL APPROACHES

THEMES

PARALYSIS

Joyce once told his brother, Stanislaus, 'the city is suffering from hemiplegia of the will' (Stuart Gilbert, ed., *The Letters of James Joyce*, Faber, 1957, revised 1966, p. 55), meaning that Dubliners were paralysed from acting or living decisively or even consciously. Elsewhere he described his intention to write *Dubliners* as the desire, 'to betray the soul of that hemiplegia or paralysis which many consider a city'. This theme is evident in every story of the collection, in Eveline's inability to leave Dublin, in Little Chandler's frustration at being trapped in an unglamorous and intellectually stifling job and marriage, and in the futility and insignificance of the election in 'Ivy Day in the Committee Room'. From the first sentence of 'The Sisters' to the last sentence of 'The Dead', the sense of paralysis is evoked throughout, and in many different forms: sexual, political, social, moral, cultural, emotional.

The reasons for Joyce's vision of Dublin paralysed are not clear. It is possible that he represents the city in this way out of cynicism, out of his own frustration at the limitations of Dublin life. It is also possible that he is offering solutions, or at least identifying the causes of Dublin's paralysis. In most stories, for instance, there is a strong emphasis on the lack of spiritual or artistic values. Money is more important to the characters than values. Mrs Kearney embodies this materialist attitude, as do Lenehan and Corley, and Father Purdon in 'Grace' preaches on spiritual accountancy, suggesting that even religion has become a form of materialism. The lower middle and middle classes represented in *Dubliners* are debased and materialist, and have no experience of spirituality or art in any real form.

The only spiritual experience in the collection is Gabriel Conroy's vision of the snow falling across all of Ireland and over the grave of the heroic Michael Furey. The revelation inspires Gabriel to decide to embark on a **symbolic** journey to the west of Ireland. What causes the change in

Gabriel's outlook is his apprehension of himself as a pathetic being and, whereas similar thoughts occur to Little Chandler, Farrington, and perhaps Mr Duffy, in Gabriel's case the realisation comes as a dramatic **epiphany**, in the contrast between his feelings for his wife and the intense, romantic passion of Michael Furey. The story of Furey's love makes Gabriel see his own feelings as debased and corrupt, leading to his recognition of the need to transform himself. 'The Dead' may be offering a solution, therefore, to the paralysis of will that afflicts Dublin.

GROWTH AND MATURITY

This theme is also central to Joyce's later work *A Portrait of the Artist as a Young Man* (1916), in which the life of Stephen Dedalus is traced from his first childhood perceptions and memories to his self-proclaimed role as the artist and conscience of his race when he graduates from university. In that novel, Joyce traces the emotional, intellectual and spiritual journey of Dedalus from innocence to maturity.

A Portrait of the Artist as a Young Man is often referred to as a **Bildungsroman**, a formation novel, which follows the development of the central character through childhood to adulthood. In the *Dubliners* stories a similar process can be discerned. The characters in the first three stories are young enough still to entertain hopes and dreams of their adult lives and the adventures and experiences they might have. As the characters grow older in each story, however, we see the transition from youthful hope to adult despair, and perhaps in middle age to resignation. As discussed above, the final story may take the collection further by offering the possibility of revelation and transformation. One of the most interesting facets of the collection is that although different characters appear in each story, there are similarities between them which can make them comparable as earlier or later versions of each other.

DUBLIN

Dublin was the subject of all of Joyce's novels and the play, *Exiles* (written 1915, published 1918), as well as the *Dubliners* collection, despite the fact that, for most of his life, Joyce did not live in Dublin but on the Continent. Part of the reason why he wrote so much about Dublin is that he felt he knew Dublin better than any other place, and he did have a very detailed knowledge of the city and its people.

At the turn of the century, Dublin was still small enough to be familiar and relatively knowable. Moreover, Joyce believed that Dubliners had much more in common as a group of people than Parisians or Londoners. To impress upon the reader a sense of the familiarity of Dublin, Joyce often had characters from one story or novel reappear in others. Kernan, Cunningham and others from 'Grace' appear in *Ulysses*, for example, and Holohan is mentioned in 'Two Gallants' and then emerges as a character in 'A Mother'. Joyce also considered Dublin one of the most eminent and historically important cities in Europe, and wondered why it appeared so little and so rarely in European, or even English literature. His writings are then a celebration of Dublin as a city worthy of modern literary representation, even if his representations of Dublin are not entirely flattering.

TECHNIQUES

STREAM OF CONSCIOUSNESS / INTERIOR MONOLOGUE

Stream of consciousness is the technique of presenting the reader with the contents and thought processes of a character's mind by reproducing the sense of ideas, perceptions and thoughts flowing through consciousness. Joyce perfected the technique to great effect in *A Portrait of the Artist as a Young Man*, in presenting the sensory perceptions of a child, for example, and in *Ulysses*, in Molly Bloom's soliloquy at the end.

In *Dubliners* he uses it to indicate the point of view of each particular character. In 'The Dead', for example, we are witness throughout to Gabriel's inner thoughts and desires:

> Gabriel's warm trembling fingers tapped the cold pane of the window. How cool it must be outside! How pleasant it would be to walk out alone, first along by the river and then through the park! The snow would be lying on the branches of the trees and forming a bright cap on the top of the Wellington Monument. How much more pleasant it would be there than at the supper-table! (pp. 218–9)

Here the narrative is made up of third person description – 'Gabriel's warm trembling fingers tapped the cold pane of the window' – and Gabriel's inner thoughts – 'How cool it must be outside!' The combination allows for the realistic presentation of the events which make up the story and the impressionistic representation of the consciousness of the characters.

Epiphany

Joyce called his early stories **epiphanies**. The word epiphany means a manifestation or revelation of truth, or in the sense of story-telling, the presentation of an aspect of truth or reality. The *Dubliners* stories are then intended to be fragments of truth, and this follows the tradition of story-telling in its quest for the epiphanic quality of revealing truth through a **symbolic** fragment. There is a strong spiritual dimension to the epiphanic techniques used in *Dubliners* too. Joyce says as much in his commentaries upon *Dubliners* to his brother Stanislaus:

> Don't you think ... there is a certain resemblance between the mystery of the Mass and what I am trying to do? I mean that I am trying ... to give some kind of intellectual pleasure or spiritual enjoyment by converting the bread of everyday life into something that has a permanent artistic life of its own ... for their mental, moral and spiritual uplift.

By presenting everyday moments of disappointment, happiness or realisation as spiritual revelations, Joyce is endowing the ordinary with extraordinary significance. Think of the moments in *Dubliners* when revelations occur – in the conclusion to 'Araby', for example, when the boy realises that the exotic enticement of the bazaar has been merely an advertising trick. Such an ordinary disappointment is transformed in *Dubliners* into a life-changing experience, a moment of profound spiritual revelation.

Language and style

The language of *Dubliners* is noteworthy for several reasons. Firstly, Joyce frequently inserts **colloquial** and slang words which convey the impression of a distinct locality with its own traditions of communicating and meaning. Dublin slang is not the only form used however. There are also slang terms from Cockney, French and other parts of Ireland used in the text. Secondly, Joyce occasionally indicates differences in the accents of the characters, thereby implying class and regional differences, such as Lily's pronouncing Gabriel's surname with three syllables – Con-er-oy. Some of the characters have Gaelic intonations to their speech patterns, rather than more Anglicised forms. Thirdly, the vocabulary used in some of the stories may be understood as mimicking the speech patterns, and linguistic abilities, of the characters, as is the case in 'Clay'. Fourthly, like other modern short story writers – Hemingway being a prime example – Joyce strips the language of his stories occasionally to the bare minimum of description. Consider this example from 'Two Gallants': 'They walked along Nassau Street and then turned into Kildare Street' (p. 57). Short stories need to be economical with words, and Joyce achieves a balance between providing terse, adjective-free prose and filling passages with images, **symbols** and metaphors necessary to convey particular effects. The impression of staleness and inert consciousness conveyed by the rich description of the houses and interiors at the beginning of 'Araby' provides an illustration of this latter point.

DESCRIPTION, IMAGERY AND SYMBOLISM

The imagery and description used in *Dubliners* is an essential device in forming the impressions and effects which the stories have on readers. 'Araby' conveys the impression of darkness, for example, culminating in the narrator, 'Gazing up into the darkness' of the bazaar (p. 36). This impression is created by using images for darkness and dullness throughout the story, such as 'sombre' houses, 'feeble lanterns', 'darkness' pervading halls and streets, and the narrator's occasional suggestions that he cannot see properly. Similarly, 'Counterparts' communicates to the reader a sense of violence and frustration by using various words and phrases for anger and physical violence, such as: 'The bell rang furiously'; '*Blast him!*' (both p. 95), 'a spasm of rage' (p. 96); 'bring his fist down on something violently' (p. 100). 'Counterparts' concludes, of course, with the main character, Farrington, beating his young son. Imagery is also used in *Dubliners* to convey the proper sense of movement or manner, as with this image from 'Two Gallants': 'Corley swung his head to and fro as if to toss aside an insistent insect' (p. 57). Here the simile of tossing his head like 'an insistent insect' is used to express an image of Corley's movement.

Imagery is also used to treat the gestures or actions of a character with humour: 'His conversation, which was serious, took place at intervals in his great brown beard' (p. 153). Joyce often uses imagery to make caricatures of certain characters, by repeating various synonyms for smallness to form a sense of Maria's diminutive stature in 'Clay', for example. Maria is obviously not a large person, but the constant repetition of imagery denoting smallness indicates that Joyce is caricaturing her features. In this way, the imagery does not just adorn the language of the story and make it more pleasurable to read, but it performs a vital function in shaping perceptions of characters and events in the stories.

In some stories, word pictures are repeated as a structuring device. In 'The Dead', for example, the image of Gabriel looking at the snow outside occurs at regular intervals through the story until the story closes with the image of snow falling all over Ireland. The regular occurrence of this image gives the reader the impression of Gabriel looking out at the snow for a way of escaping from his own sense of embarrassment and his sense of difference from others. The snow represents something which is beautiful and attractive to Gabriel, and we find him on several occasions in the story staring out of the window and imagining the snow falling across the park, the city, and finally the whole of Ireland. The repetition of images of snow outside, then, structures the story to build up to a dramatic climax in which Gabriel's life seems to be on the edge of a momentous decision or change.

Symbolism is also widely used in *Dubliners*. A symbol is a word or image which stands for something else, such as a dove symbolising peace. There are many conventional symbols in *Dubliners*, such as worms and clay for death, dirt and squalor for sin, and coins for corruption. These symbols help to shape the central theme of each story. The coin which Corley acquires in 'Two Gallants' suggest that he is corrupt and is involved in something dishonourable. So too, in 'Clay', the clay which Maria touches when she is blindfolded in the Hallowe'en game suggests the gloom and death which shadow Maria throughout the story.

The characters also read and understand the symbolism which abounds in their daily rituals and occasional celebrations. In 'Clay' the characters believe that various objects symbolise their destinies in the future, such as the ring symbolising marriage, the prayer book representing the convent, water for long life, and clay symbolising death. In 'Grace' the characters gathered around Tom Kernan's bedside acknowledge differences in the symbolic significance of candles between the Catholic and Protestant faiths, while the controversy over Father Flynn in 'The Sisters' centres on the symbolic meaning of the chalice and blessed wine, which Catholics believe symbolises the blood of Christ. The characters interpret and employ symbols in their everyday lives.

Political symbols are apparent in many of the stories, in a straightforward way in 'Ivy Day in the Committee Room', but also in more obscure ways in other stories. The following image from 'Two Gallants' invokes a poignant symbol of Irish national identity, the harp, being treated carelessly by modern indifference, and being indifferent itself:

> Not far from the porch of the club a harpist stood in the roadway, playing to a little ring of listeners. He plucked at the wires heedlessly, glancing quickly from time to time at the face of each new-comer and from time to time, wearily also, at the sky. His harp too, heedless that her coverings had fallen about her knees, seemed weary alike of the eyes of strangers and of her master's hands. (pp. 57–8)

This image suggests that the lack of enthusiasm for the national cause is a part of the wider sterility and paralysis of Dublin life at the turn of the century. Such symbolism is used widely throughout *Dubliners*, and gives key indications of the significance of the events and characters represented in the stories.

The general theme of paralysis, which pervades each of the stories and makes them coherent as a collection, is conveyed through a series of symbols. The paralysis of Dublin and Irish life is symbolised in *Dubliners* by Father Flynn's stroke at the beginning of the collection, by the headstones and graveyards of the final paragraph of the collection, and by many images and characters in between. Joyce's Dublin is populated by politicians with no interest in politics, priests who are mistaken for actors and young men and women who dream of nothing other than leaving the country. Those who dream of getting out symbolise the difficulty of living in Dublin, and in the later stories that dream has turned into the feeling of being trapped, which symbolises the death of all hope. Maria in 'Clay' and Mr Duffy in 'A Painful Case' are two characters who have become trapped in a deadly routine of living without passion or hope in Dublin.

The last stories, 'Grace' and 'The Dead', begin to symbolise resurrection or new life, with Tom Kernan visiting a church with the promise of turning over a new life, and Gabriel Conroy deciding to 'set out on his journey westward' (p. 255), symbolising a new beginning for him. The symbolic shape of *Dubliners*, then, is to begin with the recognition of paralysis in childhood, the experience of envy at the attractions of life outside a paralysed Dublin and Ireland in youth, the feeling of being trapped in maturity, and the final hint that there might be a way out of paralysis towards the end of the collection.

PART FOUR

TEXTUAL ANALYSIS

IMAGERY AND PARALYSIS ('ARABY', PAGE 29)

North Richmond Street, being blind, was a quiet street except at the hour when the Christian Brothers' School set the boys free. An uninhabited house of two storeys stood at the blind end, detached from its neighbours in a square ground. The other houses of the street, conscious of decent lives within them, gazed at one another with brown imperturbable faces.

The former tenant of our house, a priest, had died in the back drawing-room. Air, musty from having been long enclosed, hung in all the rooms, and the waste room behind the kitchen was littered with old useless papers. Among these I found a few paper-covered books, the pages of which were curled and damp: *The Abbot*, by Walter Scott, *The Devout Communicant* and *The Memoirs of Vidocq*. I liked the last best because its leaves were yellow. The wild garden behind the house contained a central apple-tree and a few straggling bushes under one of which I found the late tenant's rusty bicycle-pump. He had been a very charitable priest; in his will he had left all his money to institutions and the furniture of his house to his sister.

Joyce's stories are preoccupied with the theme of paralysis, the paralysis of the city and all of the people who live in it (see Paralysis in Themes). He conveys this theme not just by inventing characters who are trapped in the same material or mental circumstances for the rest of their lives, like Eveline or Little Chandler, but by deploying a set of images which communicate to the reader an atmosphere and impression of entrapment or stagnancy.

In the first paragraph of the passage above, for example, Joyce gives the streets and houses of Dublin human attributes in order to construct the impression that the very buildings and objects of Dublin are paralysed. North Richmond Street, which is a cul-de-sac, is described as 'blind', implying that it is physically impaired or disabled, that it is trapped in darkness. The house in which the story begins is described as 'uninhabited' and 'detached', suggesting the emptiness and loneliness the boy will come to feel himself at the end of the story. And the houses are said to be 'conscious of decent lives within them' and gazing 'at one another with brown imperturbable faces'. It seems that the city itself is a living being, and that it, like all of its inhabitants, is devoid of passion, excitement, hope, or warmth.

While the first paragraph has established the impression that the places in which Dubliners live are paralysed and paralysing, the second paragraph adds to the imagery of stagnancy and decay. The words 'died', 'musty', 'enclosed', 'hung', 'waste', 'littered', 'old', 'useless', 'curled and damp', 'straggling' and 'rusty' contribute to the sense that Dubliners are stifled from growing, and are limited in the lives which they can lead. The boy narrator is already caught up in this stunted life, surrounded as he is by the memories of an unnamed dead priest and the corroding, yellow-leaved books. The imagery which this paragraph sets up is particularly poignant because it contrasts with the boy's hopes and dreams of exotic love and prefigures the deflation of those dreams in the conclusion when the boy realises that the exoticism promised by the Araby bazaar is hollow and superficial.

An atmosphere can be conveyed effectively in a short story by placing words with similar meanings or senses in close proximity to one another, and by attributing these meanings or senses to particular objects or characters. The story would not work in the same way if Joyce had described the street as a cul-de-sac, and the house as 'pleasant' and 'close to its neighbours', or if he had used words like 'fresh', 'wonderful', 'new', 'clean' or 'sparkling' in the second paragraph instead of the images of decay and stagnancy. The imagery which he uses in the passage above contributes to establishing the theme of paralysis and entrapment in the minds of readers, and plays a key role in forming an impression of Dublin life from the point of view of the characters who are trapped in it (see Description, Imagery and Symbolism in Techniques).

REPETITION AND LANGUAGE ('CLAY', PAGES 111–2)

> When the cook told her everything was ready she went into the women's room and
> began to pull the big bell. In a few minutes the women began to come in by twos and
> threes, wiping their steaming hands in their petticoats and pulling down the sleeves
> of their blouses over their red steaming arms. They settled down before their huge
> mugs which the cook and the dummy filled up with hot tea, already mixed with milk

and sugar in huge tin cans. Maria superintended the distribution of the barmbrack and saw that every woman got her four slices. There was a great deal of laughing and joking during the meal. Lizzie Fleming said Maria was sure to get the ring and, though Fleming had said that for so many Hallow Eves, Maria had to laugh and say she didn't want any ring or man either; and when she laughed her grey-green eyes sparkled with disappointed shyness and the tip of her nose nearly met the tip of her chin. Then Ginger Mooney lifted up her mug of tea and proposed Maria's health while all the other women clattered with their mugs on the table, and said she was sorry she hadn't a sup of porter to drink it in. And Maria laughed again till the tip of her nose nearly met the tip of her chin and till her minute body nearly shook itself asunder because she knew that Mooney meant well though, of course, she had the notions of a common woman.

There are many passages in *Dubliners*, including the much celebrated conclusion of 'The Dead', which use the repetition of nouns and adjectives in order to insist on a particular visual effect. In the case of the above passage, we cannot help but have the impression of women, laughing, mugs of tea, steaming, the ring, and Maria laughing 'till the tip of her nose nearly met the tip of her chin', which is repeated several times through the story. Joyce repeats words twice or three times, always rearranging them, and applying them to different characters or objects, which prevents the repetition becoming excessive or monotonous.

There is another way of approaching the use of repetition in 'Clay', which is to see repetition as a device intended to mimic the language of the character (see Language and Style in Techniques). Repetition in 'Clay' is composed almost entirely of small words like 'mug', 'tea', 'laugh' and 'nose'. The effect of this device is to convey the impression that the vocabulary and mental dexterity of the character is limited. This is not to say that Maria is stupid, but that the language which she uses is restricted and indicates a contracted, stifled mind. Everything about Maria is small, and there are many synonyms for small used in the story, all implying the compact and constricted world which she inhabits. This may, of course, be a part of the larger picture of paralysis and narrowness which 'Clay' and the *Dubliners* collection represents (see Paralysis in Themes).

SOCIAL DETAIL ('A LITTLE CLOUD', PAGES 77–8)

He emerged from under the feudal arch of the King's Inns, a neat modest figure, and walked swiftly down Henrietta Street. The golden sunset was waning and the air had grown sharp. A horde of grimy children populated the street. They stood or ran in the roadway or crawled up the steps before the gaping doors or squatted like mice upon the thresholds. Little Chandler gave them no thought. He picked his way deftly through all that minute vermin-like life and under the shadow of the gaunt spectral mansions in which the old nobility of Dublin had roistered. No memory of the past touched him, for his mind was full of a present joy.

He had never been in Corless's but he knew the value of the name. He knew that people went there after the theatre to eat oysters and drink liqueurs; and he had heard that the waiters there spoke French and German. Walking swiftly by at night he had seen cabs drawn up before the door and richly dressed ladies, escorted by cavaliers, alight and enter quickly. They wore noisy dresses and many wraps. Their faces were powdered and they caught up their dresses, when they touched earth, like alarmed Atalantas. He had always passed without turning his head to look. It was his habit to walk swiftly in the street even by day and whenever he found himself in the city late at night he hurried on his way apprehensively and excitedly. Sometimes, however, he courted the causes of his fear. He chose the darkest and narrowest streets and, as he walked boldly forward, the silence that was spread about his footsteps troubled him, the wandering silent figures troubled him; and at times a sound of low fugitive laughter made him tremble like a leaf.

Dubliners abounds with depictions of the daily social, cultural and economic life of the city's inhabitants. For the most part the stories concern the lower middle class and middle class in Dublin society, and only occasionally do they stray into other class strata, in 'The Dead' or in 'After the Race', for example. Often the stories do not just depict the life of Dubliners in particular social circumstances, but indicate their perspectives, or their points of view.

In the passage above, taken from 'A Little Cloud', the attitudes of the main character, Little Chandler, to social class are indicated throughout. He is described as a 'neat, modest figure', which may be his own self-image. He encounters children in the slums of North Dublin as he passes on his way to meeting his glamorous friend. Here the children are described as 'a horde', 'grimy', populating (crowding?) the street. There follow a series of images of the children as vermin – they 'crawled' and 'squatted like mice'. These unusual descriptions of children are not the objective representations of the author but are intended to indicate Little Chandler's view.

Note the contrast between his view of the children to whom he gives 'no thought' in the first paragraph and his view of the upper-class ladies in the second paragraph, who are associated with positive images of theatre, eating, drinking, dresses, waiters speaking foreign languages, carriages, and swift, quick and light movements. The second paragraph goes on to give us the narrator's description of Little Chandler walking through the city, sometimes cautiously and fearfully, sometimes walking the narrowest, darkest streets deliberately to experience the fear of 'low fugitive laughter' and 'the silence that was spread about his footsteps'. The passage quoted shows Little Chandler caught between his hatred of the poor and his admiration of the rich, in a city in which the worlds of the poor and the rich live side by side. Little Chandler wanders through the streets of poverty and of riches, courting the fear and excitement of both, but stifled by the fact that he belongs to neither class.

PART FIVE

BACKGROUND

JAMES JOYCE

James Augustine Joyce was born on February 2nd 1882 in Rathgar, a Victorian suburb of Dublin (see Chronology). He was the oldest of ten surviving children born to John and Mary Jane Joyce. The Joyces were a Catholic middle class family, much like many of the families depicted in *Dubliners*. John Joyce was a rate collector whose earnings at the beginnings of his career allowed the family to live in comfortable suburbs to the south of Dublin, including the seaside town of Bray (see Maps).

James Joyce had a governess, Mrs Dante Conway, in his childhood, and in 1888 went to the prestigious Clongowes Wood College, a Jesuit school. His father was unable to manage the family finances, however, and the family slipped further into poverty, taking up rented tenement accommodation in north Dublin. The lack of money meant that James could not be kept in a fee-paying school, and he was moved instead to a Christian Brothers' School. In 1893, a Jesuit teacher who remembered Joyce's ability at Clongowes got him a free place at Belvedere College, also run by Jesuits, and this led Joyce on to further education in University College Dublin in 1898. There he delighted in reading foreign literature, in particular the work of Henrik Ibsen, who was denounced at that time as an immoral playwright. At the University he argued for drama which showed real life in **symbolic** shape, and he began to write short poems and prose pieces, which he called '**epiphanies**'.

In June 1902 Joyce graduated, now fluent in English, Irish, Latin, French, Italian and German, and possessing some Norwegian. Following this he began to take Medical Studies, in Dublin and then in Paris, but this idea was soon thwarted by his mother's illness, which brought him back to Dublin. After his mother's death in 1903, Joyce began to publish some of his stories in Irish journals. In 1904 Joyce met Nora Barnacle, and they travelled on the Continent for some time before ending up in Trieste. From there Joyce sent twelve stories of *Dubliners* to Grant Richards in 1905 for publication but, although Richards agreed to publish the stories, the printer denounced the stories as immoral and refused to print them.

Dubliners was again submitted for publication in 1907 with Richards, but was refused, following which it was accepted and then rejected by Maunsel and Co., and was finally accepted again by Richards and published in London in 1914. After 1912 Joyce and Nora never really returned to Dublin. Instead, they stayed in Europe, moving between Trieste and Zurich, and then to Paris. *Dubliners* was followed by *A Portrait of the Artist as a Young Man*, which Joyce had been writing since 1904. In 1922 *Ulysses* was published in France, but was banned in the USA until 1934 and in the UK until 1936. In 1939 Joyce's longest and most complex novel, *Finnegans Wake* was published, two years before Joyce's death in 1941 in Zürich.

Throughout this time Joyce and Nora Barnacle lived in poverty, and Joyce was troubled with severe eyesight problems. Joyce had also experienced many problems publishing his work, and his novel *Ulysses* was banned from all English-speaking countries until the American version was published in 1934. Oliver St John Gogarty was to remark of *Ulysses* that it had been 'written on the toilet walls of Dublin', which indicates the reaction which Joyce's blend of realism, **irony** and satire could provoke.

In his own lifetime, Joyce's literary abilities were barely recognised, and certainly not in his own country, where his critical attitudes towards the dominant beliefs and customs of the time earned him few admirers. Ironically, he is now the subject of many tourist industry projects in Ireland, including the *Ulysses* tour of Dublin.

His other works

Joyce's early writings experiment with the naturalist form, attempting to fuse **realist** narrative with the presentation of individual consciousness. The stories in *Dubliners* are both detailed descriptions of the social fabric of a modern city and investigations of the individual experiences of the city. To achieve this fusion of realism and consciousness Joyce employed what became known as the **stream of consciousness** technique. He presents the inner perceptions and thoughts of a character as the interior monologue of the narrative (see Stream of Consciousness in Techniques).

Although this technique is used occasionally in *Dubliners*, Joyce developed and exploited its potential fully in *A Portrait of the Artist as a*

Young Man. In this semi-autobiographical novel, Joyce shows us the development of the artist, Stephen Dedalus, from his first memories or conscious thoughts through his childhood to his graduation from university. The novel reflects the growing consciousness of Dedalus in its shifts of tone and style, from the childlike simplicity and sensory perceptions at the beginning of the novel to Stephen's own self-conscious, and highly stylised, intellectual proclamations at the end of the novel.

Dedalus also appears as one of the main characters in Joyce's *Ulysses*, a novel which took the experimentation with style and language into new dimensions. Not only is *Ulysses* brimming with literary, artistic and cultural allusions, but it also alters styles of writing, and linguistic and formal patterns, throughout the narrative. It follows the adventures and thoughts of Stephen Dedalus and Leopold Bloom through one day, June 16th 1904 (the day on which Joyce had first walked with Nora Barnacle through the streets of Dublin). Many of the characters who appear in *Dubliners* and *A Portrait of the Artist as a Young Man* reappear in *Ulysses*, such as Miss Kearney, Dante Riordan and Gabriel Conroy.

Much of the social detail of Joyce's writings is derived from his extensive knowledge and memory of Dublin life and Joyce boasted that he could remember the names of every proprietor of, and all the goods stocked in, every shop on the main thoroughfares of Dublin. This enabled him to write detailed portraits of the city, including dense allusions to the actual social, cultural and political world in which his fictional characters were depicted living and working. In *Ulysses*, Joyce tested formal conventions by setting the narrative within innovative formal structures, such as the unpunctuated final chapter in which Molly Bloom's thoughts are allowed to flow uninterrupted and uninhibited.

In his final novel, *Finnegans Wake*, Joyce probed further into the relationship between language and form. In particular, the relationship between language and meaning is a key concern of the novel. Joyce creates a hybrid language out of words forced together with other words, or altered to bring out hidden rhythms or senses. The opening lines of the novel give an indication of the kind of word play that Joyce pursued in *Finnegans Wake*:

> riverrun, past Eve and Adam's, from swerve of shore to bend of bay, brings us by a commodius vicus of recirculation back to Howth Castle and Environs.

> Sir Tristram, violer d'amores, fr'over the short sea, had passencore rearrived from North Armorica on this side the scraggy isthmus of Europe Minor to wielderfight his penisolate war … (p. 7)

Finnegans Wake is the most allusive, dense and difficult of Joyce's writings. Although he is known primarily for his achievements in prose fiction, Joyce also wrote a play, *Exiles*, and poetry, as well as political and cultural critiques in essay form. Parts of the first version of *A Portrait of the Artist as a Young Man*, entitled *Stephen Hero*, were published in 1944, three years after his death.

HISTORICAL BACKGROUND

POLITICS

For much of the latter half of the nineteenth century the majority of the Irish electorate had tried to persuade the British Parliament to allow Ireland to govern itself. These campaigns for home rule were led by Charles Stewart Parnell, an Irish M.P., who led the Irish Parliamentary Party in their bid to achieve a limited form of independence by constitutional means. But Parnell's political career was ruined in 1890 when he was cited as a co-respondent in the O'Shea divorce case, and British and Irish political and church leaders denounced his involvement in the affair. He died in 1891 while struggling to repair his reputation, and his death weakened the campaign for home rule severely. The result was that Irish political life was without clear direction throughout the 1890s and the first decade of the twentieth century.

This sense of aimlessness and the lack of strong political leadership is made apparent in *Dubliners*, firstly by the atmosphere of paralysis which pervades the stories, and secondly by the lack of enthusiasm for politics shown specifically in 'Ivy Day in the Committee Room'. As Frank O'Connor has pointed out, the 'pok' sound of the corks popping out of the three beer bottles mimics the sound of three gunshots fired over Parnell's coffin (Frank O'Connor, *The Lonely Voice*, Bantam, 1963, p. 190). The fact that they are beer bottle corks rather than gunshots implies that the honour and respect owed to Parnell is given only half-heartedly and without genuine feeling.

The time in which the stories of *Dubliners* are set saw the revival of interest in Irish culture and fashions among Irish people who had turned in the past to England as a cultural model. Hence we can see in many of the stories, notably 'A Mother' and 'The Dead', discussions of what it means to participate in this revival. But Joyce depicts the nationalism of his middle class characters in very **ironic** terms, as in the reference in 'A Mother' to Mrs Kearney taking advantage of her daughter's 'Irish' name, and to her daughter's nationalism as an exchange of Irish picture postcards.

RELIGION

In Joyce's time, Catholicism formed the religion of the majority of the population in Ireland (as it still does now). In the seventeenth and eighteenth centuries English colonial rulers had pursued a policy of stamping out Catholicism, prohibiting Catholic ceremonies, churches and schools, and forbidding Catholics from owning property above a certain size. In the nineteenth century, some reforms were introduced and many of the more repressive laws were repealed. Catholics acquired property rights and the right to vote in elections. As a result, the Catholic middle class grew rapidly, and by the end of the nineteenth century much of Ireland's commercial, land and industrial wealth lay in Catholic people's hands.

There were still some anomalies in the treatment of Catholics, and we see this in *Dubliners* in the mention of pro-Cathedrals – that is, churches which had to act as cathedrals because the city's cathedrals were reserved for the Protestant Church of Ireland – and in the reference to the University question, which concerned the provision of university education within a Catholic framework (Trinity College in Dublin was perceived to be, and to a large extent was, a Protestant institution).

Catholicism is woven into the fabric of the daily lives of the Dubliners, with priests appearing regularly throughout the stories. But Joyce often treats his priest characters **ironically**. The priests who appear in *Dubliners* are mostly dead ('The Sisters', 'Araby'), 'bad' (Father Keon in 'Ivy Day in the Committee Room'), or too worldly (Father Purdon in 'Grace'). More importantly, Joyce treats the religious beliefs and pretensions of his other characters ironically, as is clearly evident in the discussion about popes and their mottoes in 'Grace'. When Protestantism appears in the stories, it is often as the butt of Catholic jokes and jibes, as when Mr Browne in 'The Dead' is described by Mary Jane as being 'of the other persuasion' (p. 222). The awareness in the Catholic characters of Protestants as 'others' indicates the dominance of Catholicism, almost to the point of ridiculing all other beliefs.

DUBLIN

In the eighteenth century, under colonialism, Dublin had remained the political and cultural capital of Ireland, with its own parliament and its own civic and cultural centres. But the Act of Union of Great Britain and Ireland in 1800 abolished the Dublin parliament and subsequently Ireland's political and cultural centre lay in London. The result was that Dublin was a city with a confused identity. The confusion, about whether it is a provincial city, like Cardiff, Manchester or Newcastle, or a national capital, like London, Paris or Rome, is evident throughout *Dubliners*.

Because Dublin is merely a centre for some administrative and business interests, without its own government or cultural centre, it is a place in which many of its inhabitants feel trapped. Eveline, Little Chandler, Farrington and other 'Dubliners' are all frustrated by the meanness and narrowness of Dublin life. In 'After the Race', Jimmy Doyle learns that Dublin can only be a playground for the European rich. It can never compete with Paris or London. There is a sense throughout *Dubliners*, then, that Dublin is just the provincial sub-station of a bigger power. The signs of its subservience are written on its walls, such as 'London, E.C.' (p. 173) beside the name of Mr Kernan's firm, and are evident in the pervasive feeling that to be glamorous, like Ignatius Gallagher in 'A Little Cloud', one has to leave Dublin. In 1922, with the victory of nationalism in the south of Ireland, Dublin became the political centre of Ireland again, but Joyce's Dublin is a city in limbo, without a clear purpose or sense of worth.

THE IRISH SHORT STORY

Although the tradition of oral storytelling has a long history in Ireland, dating back to ancient times when the storyteller (*sgéalaí* for long epic tales, *seanchaí* for shorter tales) held an important place in the Celtic social structure, the Irish written short story tradition dates to the early nineteenth century. In the early part of the nineteenth century Irish writers such as Gerald Griffin, William Carleton and the Banim brothers had collected and written tales, mostly either comic or horrific, about provincial and rural life in Ireland and published them for English readers. They can be seen as servicing the need among educated English readers to be entertained by strange and exotic cultures, part of the same pursuit of the exotic that we can see filtering into the lives of Dubliners in stories like 'Araby' and 'After the Race'. There is a concerted attempt in their writings to explain Irish habits, speech-patterns and social idiosyncracies for an English reader.

In the last decade of the nineteenth century, however, Irish writers began to write and collect short tales and stories and publish them for Irish readers. Writers such as W.B. Yeats, Lady Gregory and George Moore published short fiction and collections of ancient and folklore tales, and they did so with the aim of communicating to Irish readers and instilling a passion for Irish culture in educated Irish people. By far the most important antecedent in the Irish short story tradition for Joyce was George Moore. In 1903 Moore published his collection of short stories entitled *The Untilled Field*. Moore had originally entitled his collection *A Portrait of Ireland*, and intended the collection to capture a view of Irish life at the end of the nineteenth century. *The Untilled Field* as a title may be read as allegorical of Ireland, as indeed may the stories themselves be read as allegories. If Ireland is 'an untilled field' it is either being neglected and wasted, and is a resource not yet realised, or it is a barren, sterile land, not worth tilling. Moore's stories often imply criticisms of Irish life, and depict a world stunted and unable to grow. In 'Home Sickness', for example, an Irish emigrant, James Bryden, returns from America to recover in his native land from ill health, but finds all the things which made him leave Ireland in the first place – the lack of opportunity, the submission of the people to the authority of the church, and the lack of will among the people to change their ways. The contrast between stale, paralysed Ireland and the energetic, modernising America leads him to depart for America again.

Moore was influenced by Turgenev to use devices such as telescoping time into flashbacks and setting up **antitheses** within a story between two different ways of life. Similarly, Joyce brought European short story devices into his writing from the French writer, Guy de Maupassant, and the Russian Anton Chekhov. Chekhov's stories, for example, prefigure Joyce's *Dubliners* in the focus on the lives of the lower middle and middle class strata of provincial Russian society. Together these writers represent a powerful shift away from the ghost stories, mythic tales and comic yarns which dominated Irish storytelling in the early nineteenth century, and brought to fruition an Irish short story genre which told stories about ordinary, provincial life. Whereas Moore's collection was focused entirely on the rural population of Ireland, Joyce's collection was centred exclusively on Dublin. Joyce made the move to the urban in reaction to the peasant tales of previous writers, and as a result presents an image of Ireland almost wholly hidden from view in earlier Irish literature.

THE CULTURAL REVIVAL

The Irish revival was the period at the end of the nineteenth century and the beginning of the twentieth century which saw the emergence of new tastes in Irish readers and audiences for works of literature and culture which represented Irish life. It was promoted by organisations set up to revive and support Irish sport, language, dress, literature, drama and education, as well as other things. English colonial domination of Ireland had created a situation in which the Irish middle classes looked to England for political, cultural and social leadership and role models. But the revival changed Irish middle class tastes, and arguably paved the way for mass support of the war of independence from 1918 to 1921, which resulted in the establishment on an independent Irish state in the southern three-quarters of the island.

Joyce was not involved in the Irish literary and cultural revival in the same way as Yeats, Synge or Gregory. These writers were actively engaged in organising, presenting, writing, funding, promoting and celebrating the literature of Ireland in the 1890s and in the early decades of this century. Yeats set up theatres, societies and clubs, organised lecture tours and public meetings, and collected and published folklore tales so as to disseminate the cultural heritage which he thought fit to celebrate. Joyce, in contrast, was involved in the revival only to the extent that he published works about Ireland and Irish life, and that he influenced a generation of writers after him.

The revival does provide keys to understanding Joyce's work, however. It appears in various guises, from Miss Ivors trying to persuade Gabriel Conroy to take an interest in Irish language and culture, to the argument that has been made occasionally that certain stories in *Dubliners* are modern versions of ancient Gaelic tales. For the most part, the *Dubliners* stories seem to cast suspicion on the revival culture, with Mrs Kearney in 'A Mother' simply exploiting the revival as a means of social networking, and with the harpist in 'Two Gallants' playing this instrument (a **symbol** of the Irish nation) heedlessly, wearily, and at the door of an exclusive Unionist club. All the signs are that Irish culture is being exploited cynically by the revivalists for their own gain, or for the purpose of pleasing English audiences again. Joyce might have written works of extraordinary merit which have become the sources of Irish national pride, but he depicts the Irish revival in **ironic** terms for the most part.

MODERNISM

Modernism is a term used to describe the art and literature of the period from about 1910 to 1940, covering writers such as T.S. Eliot, Ezra Pound, Virginia Woolf, W.B. Yeats and Ford Madox Ford. Modernist literature tends to emphasise the cross-fertilisation of cultures and the increased fragmentation of perception in the modern world. In order to represent a world growing ever more complex, disparate and difficult to know, writers experimented with forms of literary representation. Rejecting traditional **realist** forms of narrative and poetic structure, modernist writers invest-igated the means of representing the inner perceptions of human consciousness. In *Ulysses*, for example, Joyce experimented with punctu-ation, rhythm, allusion and narrative perspective in order to represent the thoughts and perceptions of the mind. Although this experimentation is more evident in later works like *Ulysses* and *Finnegans Wake*, Joyce's *Dubliners* can also be considered a work of modernist literature.

For instance, in the first three stories of *Dubliners*, the perceptions, feelings and thoughts of the boy-narrators are made clear through the use of interior monologues. Similarly, as discussed in 'Textual Analysis' above, it may be that Joyce structured the language of 'Clay' in such a way as to mimic the thought patterns and self-perceptions of Maria. Of course, *Dubliners* is also modernist in its emphasis on the urban landscape as the setting, and indeed the subject, of all the stories. As is evident from the beginning of 'Araby', in which the houses and streets are depicted as living beings, the city is a character in the story, playing as much if not more of a part than Gabriel or Miss Kearney or Little Chandler.

Modernist literature focused heavily on experiences of the city space, and the result on conceptions of human life and communication of living in urban centres. The implication of modernist representations of the city is that city life produces a heightened consciousness of the relationships between individuals, and of the diversity and multiplicity of social and cultural experiences.

PART SIX

CRITICAL HISTORY

As with most innovative writers, Joyce was not received very well in his own time. To begin with, Joyce first published some of the *Dubliners* stories in Russell's journal *The Irish Homestead* in 1904. His stories were not particularly suited to the readers of the magazine, who were in the main from rural areas and fairly conservative in their literary tastes. When he tried later to publish the stories as a collection he again ran into difficulties. The printers, rather than the publishers, were the cause, refusing to set the volume when they read the sexual innuendoes and religious slurs contained in some of its stories. It was 1914 before *Dubliners* was finally published by Grant Richards, and the reviews were not favourable, most reviewers finding the stories 'plotless' or 'too cynical' for their tastes.

Although *Ulysses*, for instance, was well known in the 1920s, Joyce's literary achievements only began to be widely recognised towards the end of his life. Harry Levin did major work with his *James Joyce: A Critical Introduction* (1941), but Joyce's place in literary history was established more securely in the late 1950s and 1960s. Richard Ellmann published what is now generally regarded as the standard biography of Joyce in 1959 (revised in 1982). William York Tyndall published *A Reader's Guide to James Joyce* in 1959 also, with the intention of aiding readers to understand the textual innovations and key contexts of Joyce's work.

Dubliners was celebrated in Frank O'Connor's book on the short story, *The Lonely Voice*, in 1963, as a collection which reflected the various stages of a storyteller's craft. For O'Connor, the first few stories are 'sketches' and autobiographical fragments. In the middle of the collection are the 'very harsh naturalistic stories about Dublin middle class life'. This middle section in turn is divided into two parts, the first, like 'Two Gallants', is mock-heroic comedy, the second, like 'Counterparts', is based on **antithesis** and oppositions within the story. The final group of stories, O'Connor believes, are the most adventurous. Highly stylistic and **symbolic** representations of a multifaceted reality, and Joyce in these stories has performed perhaps the highest feat for a short story writer, having made 'tragedy out of a plate of peas and a bottle of ginger beer' (Frank O'Connor, *The Lonely Voice*, Bantam, 1963, pp. 185–95).

An oft-made argument is that *Dubliners* is a series of studies in the spiritual paralysis of a modern city, until the final story 'The Dead', which is more hopeful and accepts a new relationship with the city. Peter Costello argued that Joyce's stories were arranged to represent the passage into maturity and experience:

> The book opens in childhood with the juvenile experience of death, moves on through sexual misadventures of 'An Encounter', 'Araby' and 'Eveline', towards the maturing experiences of a young man in 'After the Race', 'Two Gallants', and 'The Boarding House'. Then follow four stories of maturity, of failed family life in 'A Little Cloud' and 'Counterparts', of sterile relations in 'Clay' and 'A Painful Case'. The last four stories move on to deal with social groups: politics in 'Ivy Day in the Committee Room', artistic life in 'A Mother' and religion in 'Grace'. (Peter Costello, *James Joyce*, Gill and Macmillan, 1980, p. 48)

Many of the critical interpretations of *Dubliners* written in the 1950s and 1960s focused on the formal structures and technical innovations of the collection, but criticism since the 1970s has moved away from formal concerns and begun to examine the social and political aspects of his work. A significant step towards these new approaches was taken by Colin MacCabe in his book, *James Joyce and the Revolution of the Word*, published in 1979. Dissenting from previous critics who argued that the meaning of each of the *Dubliners* stories could be determined in relation to the order of the collection, MacCabe argued that there was no overarching order and explanation which could determine meaning in the stories. He saw the stories instead as hybrid narratives, made up of different styles, narrative positions and forms of language, which offered various possibilities for interpretation.

MacCabe was among the first of many critics who have since written on the *Dubliners* stories in relation to its extra-literary dimensions, that is, the relationship between the stories and social and political issues. There followed in the early 1980s a series of books on Joyce's politics, including Dominic Manganiello's *Joyce's Politics* (1980), Derek Attridge and Daniel Ferrier (eds), *Post-structuralist Joyce* (1984), Suzette Henke, *Joyce and Feminism* (1984), Vicki Mahaffy, *Reauthorising Joyce* (1988), Emer Nolan, *James Joyce and Nationalism* (1995), and Vince Cheng, *Joyce, Race and*

Empire (1995). Each of these books attempts to interpret the stories in relation to their social, political and institutional contexts, focusing on issues like imperialism, socialism and feminism where Joyce's stories seem to intervene in, and interact with, these issues.

Joyce has become the subject of a large academic industry in the last twenty years. There are several academic journals dedicated to publishing essays and reviews on Joyce's works, and a number of institutions, such as the Zürich James Joyce Foundation and the James Joyce Museum in Dublin, geared towards spreading the reputation and enjoyment of Joyce's writings. His work is taught on most university curricula in English-speaking countries, and his chief writings have been available in print with various different publishers since their first publication. Joyce has also become the subject of Irish tourist industry projects to attract foreign visitors, which has spawned a whole range of commercial merchandise like T-shirts, mugs, pens and posters. One can only wonder how such a cultural icon may have been treated as the subject of one of Joyce's stories.

PART SEVEN

BROADER PERSPECTIVES

FURTHER READING

JOYCE'S OTHER WORKS

A Portrait of the Artist as a Young Man, ed. Richard Ellman (Jonathan Cape, 1968)

Ulysses (Oxford University Press, 1993)

Finnegans Wake (Faber and Faber, 1939)

Stephen Hero (Jonathan Cape, 1969)

Exiles (Triad/Panther, 1979)

James Joyce – The Critical Writings, eds, Ellsworth Mason and Richard Ellman (Cornell University Press, 1989)

Poems and Shorter Writings (Faber and Faber, 1991)

The Cat and the Devil (Faber and Faber, 1991)

BIOGRAPHY

Richard Ellmann, *James Joyce*, Oxford University Press, 1959: revised 1982

Ellmann's biography of Joyce is widely regarded as the best. Ellmann combines detailed textual analysis with discussion of the relationship between Joyce's life and his works. Like his biography of Yeats, Ellmann tends to see Joyce as an apolitical artist, striving for universal truths beyond the limited world of national politics

Peter Costello, *James Joyce*, Gill and Macmillan, 1980

Part of the 'Gill's Irish Lives' series, Costello's short book on Joyce attempts to assess his literary achievements and to relate his works to the events of his life. The focus of this book is very much on the life rather than interpretations of Joyce's writings. Costello has recently published a new, much longer biography of Joyce

JOYCE AND DUBLINERS

Don Gifford, *Joyce Annotated: Notes for 'Dubliners' and 'A Portrait'*,
University of California Press, 1982: originally 1967

> A useful companion when reading *Dubliners*, Gifford's book explains hundreds of
> references and phrases in Joyce's stories and provides maps of the routes which
> various characters take on their adventures in the city

Colin MacCabe, *James Joyce and the Revolution of the Word*, Macmillan,
1979

> A seminal study of the linguistic, social and political concerns of Joyce's work. He
> employs concepts from psychoanalytic and linguistic theories to argue that reading
> Joyce is an active process of transforming the text, rather than a passive process of
> consuming the text

Daniel R. Schwarz, ed., *James Joyce*, The Dead, St Martin's Press, 1994

> Part of the Bedford Books series which publishes the text alongside critical
> interpretations of it, this volume on 'The Dead' includes interpretations and
> approaches which use psychoanalytic, reader-response, historicist, feminist and
> deconstruction theories to explain and analyse the meanings and significance of the
> final story in *Dubliners*

THE SHORT STORY

Frank O'Connor, *The Lonely Voice*, Bantam Books, 1968: originally 1963

> A renowned Irish short story writer, O'Connor's book on the short story provides a
> useful insight into a writer's view of the genre. Where Joyce is concerned, O'Connor
> discusses the influence of George Moore on Joyce, and analyses the techniques which
> Joyce used in his story writing

Sean O'Faolain, *The Short Story*, Mercier Press, 1972: originally 1948

> Another renowned Irish short story writer with a book on the art of short story
> writing, O'Faolain discusses the craft of writing in terms of convention, subject,
> construction and language, and pays particular attention to Daudet, Chekhov and
> Maupassant. His view of Irish life as insular and stifling is very similar to Joyce's
> portrait of Dublin in the *Dubliners* stories, and makes for an interesting context in
> which to consider the Irish short story genre

Patrick Rafroidi and Terence Brown, eds, *The Irish Short Story*, Colin Smythe, 1979

> This collection of essays on the Irish short story contains discussions of individual writers as well as the theoretical and historical contexts of Irish short story writing. It is an invaluable collection of studies of the genre, and includes an essay by Donald Torchiana on 'James Joyce's Method in *Dubliners*'

LITERARY AND HISTORICAL BACKGROUND

A. Norman Jeffares, *Anglo-Irish Literature*, Macmillan, 1982

> Jeffares' study of Irish writing in English is comprehensive and detailed, and analyses the emergence of this tradition of literature from the medieval to the modern period. Joyce is discussed in a chapter in the section on modern fiction, but Jeffares also analyses Joyce's influence on Irish writing in the twentieth century

Declan Kiberd, *Inventing Ireland: The Literature of the Modern Nation*, Jonathan Cape, 1995

> References to Joyce are peppered throughout this book, which is an ambitious study of late nineteenth and twentieth century Irish literature. Kiberd places Joyce in many contexts throughout the volume and thereby provides a useful guide to the roles which Joyce played in forming and shaping twentieth century Irish literature. For Kiberd, literature offers us models for working out social and political problems, and this is an important focus in his ideas on Joyce

Robert Welch, ed., *The Oxford Companion to Irish Literature*, Oxford University Press, 1996

> This book contains entries on key Irish writers, writings, terms and concepts, and may be useful when considering Joyce in relation to the Irish literary tradition. It includes commentaries on Joyce and his works, as well as entries on each of the *Dubliners* stories

World events	Joyce's life	Other literary events
1870 Home Government Association founded		
		1872 Nietzsche, *The Birth of Tragedy*
1880 Civil disturbances in Ireland over evictions		
1882 Phoenix Park murders	**1882** James Joyce is born to Mary and John Stanislaus Joyce on February 2 in Rathgar, south Dublin	
1883 Irish terrorist bombings in London		
	1884 Nora Barnacle born on 21 March in Galway	
1886 First Home Rule Bill defeated		
	1887 Joyce family move to Bray	
	1888 James Joyce enters Clongowes Wood College, a prestigious Jesuit school	**1888** Yeats, *Fairy and Folk Tales of the Irish Peasantry*
1891 Parnell dies, disgraced and broken by an adultery scandal	**1891** Joyce has to leave Clongowes, as his father can no longer afford the school's fees	
		1892 Wilde's *Salome* is rehearsed and banned
1893 Second Home Rule Bill rejected	**1893** The Joyces return to Dublin. James and his siblings are sent to the Christian Brothers' School, so bad are the family finances. In April, however, Joyce is admitted to Belvedere College with the fees waived	
		1894 Shaw, *Arms and the Man*
	1895 Joyce enters the Sodality of the Blessed Virgin	
	1896 Joyce's first encounter with a prostitute	

World events	Joyce's life	Other literary events

1897 Academic performances win Joyce both accolades and prize money

1898 Joyce finishes at Belvedere and begins studying at University College Dublin

1899 Irish Literary Theatre founded; Ibsen, *When We Dead Awaken*; Yeats's *The Countess Cathleen* opens. It is condemned as heretical and anti-Irish

1900 Joyce has an article on Ibsen published in the *Fortnightly Review*. Ibsen writes to thank Joyce personally

1900 Oscar Wilde dies

1901 Queen Victoria dies. Edward VII is the new king

1902 Joyce graduates and leaves for Paris, where he plans to study medicine

1903 Joyce's mother is seriously ill and he returns to Dublin. She dies in August

1903 Moore, *The Untilled Field*

1904 Work starts on *Stephen Hero*. Joyce meets Nora Barnacle in June. They leave for the Continent in October, finally ending up at Pola, in what is now Croatia

1904 Abbey Theatre opens in Dublin. It becomes a focus for the Irish Revival

1905 Sinn Féin established

1905 The couple relocate to Trieste in Austro-Hungarian Empire. A son, Giorgio, is born

1906 He finishes 'The Dead', completing *Dubliners*, and begins to revise *Stephen Hero* as *A Portrait of the Artist as a Young Man*

1907 Daughter Anna Lucia is born. *Chamber Music* is published

1907 Synge, *The Playboy of the Western World*

World events	Joyce's life	Other literary events
	1909 Joyce visits Dublin and Galway	
1910 George V becomes king upon the death of Edward VII		
1912 Third Home Rule Bill introduced	**1912** He returns to Dublin and Galway with his family	
1913 Militant nationalist group the Irish Volunteers forms		
1914 War breaks out in Europe. Home Rule Bill becomes law, but is suspended whilst hostilities last	**1914** *The Egoist* publishes *Portrait* in serial form. *Dubliners* is published in June. Work starts on *Ulysses*	**1914** Shaw, *Pygmalion*
	1915 He writes *Exiles*. The family moves to Zürich	
1916 Easter Rising in Dublin. Over 500 die in six days of insurrection. The British execute 15 ringleaders, but this hardens Irish resolve to gain independence	**1916** *Portrait* published in New York	
	1917 Suffering from glaucoma, Joyce has eye surgery	**1917** Pound publishes the first of his *Cantos*
1918 The Great War ends. Anglo-Irish War begins	**1918** *Exiles* published. *The Little Review* begins to serialise *Ulysses*	
1919 IRA created from the Irish Volunteers		
	1920 The Joyces move to Paris	
1921 Anglo-Irish Treaty establishes Irish Free State, which excludes the six counties of Ulster	**1921** A court case halts serialisation of *Ulysses* in *The Little Review* on grounds of obscenity	

World events	Joyce's life	Other literary events
1922 Civil War in Ireland	**1922** *Ulysses* finally published by Sylvia Beach's Parisian bookshop Shakespeare and Company	
	1923 Joyce begins *Finnegans Wake*	**1923** Yeats awarded Nobel Prize for Literature
		1924 O'Casey's *Juno and the Paycock* produced
	1927 *Pomes Penyeach* published	
	1928 He meets Samuel Beckett	
	1929 *Our Exagmination* published	**1929** O'Casey, *The Silver Tassie*
	1931 Joyce and Nora Barnacle marry. Joyce's father dies	
	1932 A grandson, Stephen James, is born. *Ecce Puer* written	
	1934 *Ulysses* finally published in book form in the USA	**1934** Beckett, *More Pricks Than Kicks*
	1936 *Ulysses* published in the UK	
1937 Irish Free State adopts a new constitution and changes its name to Eire		
1939 World War Two begins	**1939** *Finnegans Wake* published in London and New York	**1939** Yeats dies
	1941 Joyce dies in Zürich	
	1944 *Stephen Hero* published	
1948 Republic of Ireland established, severing all links with the British monarchy		
	1951 Nora Barnacle Joyce dies in Zürich	
	1956 *Epiphanies* published	
	1968 *Giacomo Joyce* published	

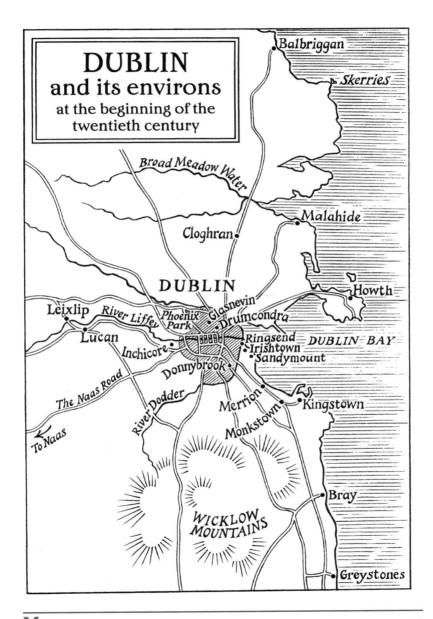

DUBLIN
and its environs
at the beginning of the
twentieth century

Balbriggan

Skerries

Broad Meadow Water

Malahide

Cloghran

DUBLIN

Glasnevin

Howth

Leixlip

River Liffey

Phoenix Park

Drumcondra

Lucan

Ringsend

Irishtown

Sandymount

DUBLIN BAY

Inchicore

Donnybrook

The Naas Road

River Dodder

Merrion

Kingstown

Monkstown

To Naas

WICKLOW MOUNTAINS

Bray

Greystones

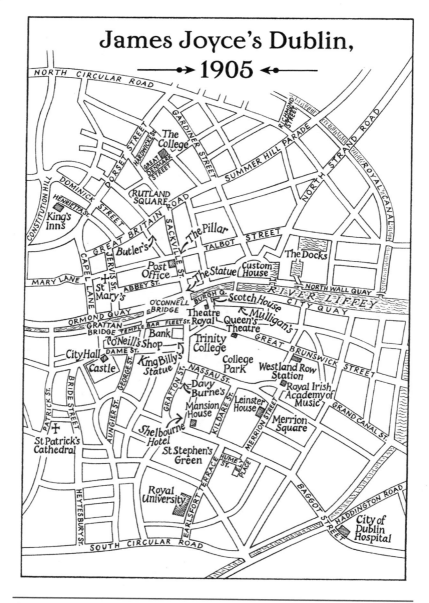

James Joyce's Dublin, 1905

allegory related to fables and parables, allegories are narratives which contain concealed second meanings which are apparent in the similarities between a character or event in the narrative and (usually) real characters and events. These similarities allow readers to follow the story in relation to the implied correspondence with the real or historical situation

antithesis opposite situations, words or phrases placed side by side. The most obvious antithesis in *Dubliners* is the opposing tastes of Gabriel Conroy and Miss Ivors in 'The Dead', with Gabriel preferring the Continent, anglophile literature and foreign languages, while Miss Ivors likes the west of Ireland, Irish literature and the Irish language

Bildungsroman formation-novel, a term which refers to the genre of fiction which features the growth of the main character from childhood through to maturity. The bildungsroman often employs the device of the interior monologue to convey the personal perceptions and subjective experiences of growing up

colloquial relaxed, everyday language, rather than formalised or conventional language. Colloquialisms in literature will often be composed of the use of 'incorrect' grammar, such as 'yous' instead of the plural 'you', and the incorporation of localised or regional language, like the words 'jackeen' or 'eejit' in Ireland. Slang is also part of colloquial language

ellipsis the omission of words or phrases from a text. This can occur for different purposes. Elliptical dots (...) are used in reporting dialogue when a character has stopped speaking in mid sentence, for example. But ellipsis can also occur when a word has been omitted for a deliberate effect, such as 'Did he ... peacefully?' in 'The Sisters' (p. 14), in which the word 'die' has been omitted by the person speaking in order to soften the effect of the question on the sister of the deceased

epiphany the presentation or revelation of truth. In storytelling, the epiphany is the dramatic revelation of the 'point' or truth of the story, but it also has a particular spiritual connotation, of being the appearance of a spiritual truth through an ordinary or banal occurrence

formalism the study of the formal features of a text, such as the language, structures and techniques of the text. It is associated specifically with a group of Russian critics in the early part of this century, but referred more generally to the tendency to study texts for their formal features alone in literary criticism

irony to say something while deliberately meaning the opposite, or to imply a different meaning by understatement and allusion. In *Dubliners*, many characters are the subject of Joyce's irony, seeming to be represented as respectable, decent people, yet intimated by the subtle use of images, speech patterns or symbols to be deplorable or, more commonly, laughable: Mrs Kearney in 'A Mother', for example, or Eliza in 'The Sisters'

malapropism from Mrs Malaprop in Sheridan's play *The Rivals*, the term 'malapropism' refers to the unwitting use of improper or muddled words, deployed by the author for comic effect. The most obvious example is Eliza's reference to 'rheumatic wheels' (p. 16) when she ought to say 'pneumatic wheels' in 'The Sisters'

modernism literary and artistic movement from about 1910 to 1940, involving writers such as Virginia Woolf, James Joyce, T.S. Eliot, Ezra Pound, W.B. Yeats, and Ford Madox Ford. The modernists experimented with the form and language of literature, turning away from the conventions of realism which had dominated European literature throughout the nineteenth century. They were particularly concerned with representing human consciousness, urban experience and cultural diaspora

parody a mock-imitation of a particular work or style of literature, with the intention of making ridiculous the conventions of that work or style. Joyce experimented with parodic techniques most successfully in *Ulysses* and *Finnegans Wake*

realism a style of literary writing in which the truth or reality about a particular kind or aspect of life is believed to be made apparent in the act of documenting and describing it. Realism was particularly prevalent in nineteenth century European literature, in which ordinary characters were depicted living in plausible, and often actual, places and conditions, and in which the language and style tends to be technically and formally unadventurous

stream of consciousness also known as interior monologue, a technique of presenting the inner thoughts and perceptions of a character as they occur to the character. Typically, the thought processes are presented as a flow of ideas, feelings and images

symbolism symbols are objects or images which come to stand for something else. A tree, for example, can symbolise strength or tradition, while white lilies conventionally symbolise death or mourning. Symbolist literature tends to emphasise the importance of using private and conventional symbols to create a wider meaning or world-view. The symbolism in *Dubliners*, for example, might be seen as responsible for creating the impression of paralysis and sterility

John Brannigan is lecturer in Irish Studies and Literary Studies at the University of Luton. He is co-editor of *Re: Joyce*, a collection of essays which reflects contemporary responses and approaches to Joyce. He has also published work on contemporary literary theories, the literature of 1950s Britain, and a number of Irish writers, including W.B. Yeats and Brendan Behan. He is currently preparing an anthology of colonial and anti-colonial writings about Ireland.

Notes

Notes

NOTES

Notes

Notes

York Notes Advanced (£3.99 each)

Margaret Atwood
The Handmaid's Tale

Jane Austen
Emma

Jane Austen
Pride and Prejudice

William Blake
Songs of Innocence and of Experience

Charlotte Brontë
Jane Eyre

Emily Brontë
Wuthering Heights

Geoffrey Chaucer
The Wife of Bath's Prologue and Tale

Joseph Conrad
Heart of Darkness

Charles Dickens
Great Expectations

F. Scott Fitzgerald
The Great Gatsby

Thomas Hardy
Tess of the d'Urbervilles

Seamus Heaney
Selected Poems

James Joyce
Dubliners

Arthur Miller
Death of a Salesman

William Shakespeare
Antony and Cleopatra

William Shakespeare
Hamlet

William Shakespeare
King Lear

William Shakespeare
The Merchant of Venice

William Shakespeare
Much Ado About Nothing

William Shakespeare
Othello

William Shakespeare
Romeo and Juliet

William Shakespeare
The Tempest

Mary Shelley
Frankenstein

Alice Walker
The Color Purple

Tennessee Williams
A Streetcar Named Desire

John Webster
The Duchess of Malfi

GCSE and equivalent levels (£3.50 each)

Harold Brighouse
Hobson's Choice

Charles Dickens
Great Expectations

Charles Dickens
Hard Times

George Eliot
Silas Marner

William Golding
Lord of the Flies

Thomas Hardy
The Mayor of Casterbridge

Susan Hill
I'm the King of the Castle

Barry Hines
A Kestrel for a Knave

Harper Lee
To Kill a Mockingbird

Arthur Miller
A View from the Bridge

Arthur Miller
The Crucible

George Orwell
Animal Farm

J.B. Priestley
An Inspector Calls

J.D. Salinger
The Catcher in the Rye

William Shakespeare
Macbeth

William Shakespeare
The Merchant of Venice

William Shakespeare
Romeo and Juliet

William Shakespeare
Twelfth Night

George Bernard Shaw
Pygmalion

John Steinbeck
Of Mice and Men

Mildred D. Taylor
Roll of Thunder, Hear My Cry

James Watson
Talking in Whispers

A Choice of Poets

Nineteenth Century Short Stories

Poetry of the First World War

Chinua Achebe
Things Fall Apart

Edward Albee
Who's Afraid of Virginia Woolf?

Maya Angelou
I Know Why The Caged Bird Sings

Jane Austen
Mansfield Park

Jane Austen
Northanger Abbey

Jane Austen
Persuasion

Jane Austen
Pride and Prejudice

Jane Austen
Sense and Sensibility

Samuel Beckett
Waiting for Godot

John Betjeman
Selected Poems

Robert Bolt
A Man for All Seasons

Charlotte Brontë
Jane Eyre

Emily Brontë
Wuthering Heights

Robert Burns
Selected Poems

Lord Byron
Selected Poems

Geoffrey Chaucer
The Franklin's Tale

Geoffrey Chaucer
The Knight's Tale

Geoffrey Chaucer
The Merchant's Tale

Geoffrey Chaucer
The Miller's Tale

Geoffrey Chaucer
The Nun's Priest's Tale

Geoffrey Chaucer
The Pardoner's Tale

Geoffrey Chaucer
Prologue to the Canterbury Tales

Samuel Taylor Coleridge
Selected Poems

Daniel Defoe
Moll Flanders

Daniel Defoe
Robinson Crusoe

Shelagh Delaney
A Taste of Honey

Charles Dickens
Bleak House

Charles Dickens
David Copperfield

Charles Dickens
Oliver Twist

Emily Dickinson
Selected Poems

John Donne
Selected Poems

Douglas Dunn
Selected Poems

George Eliot
Middlemarch

George Eliot
The Mill on the Floss

T.S. Eliot
The Waste Land

T.S. Eliot
Selected Poems

Henry Fielding
Joseph Andrews

E.M. Forster
Howards End

E.M. Forster
A Passage to India

John Fowles
The French Lieutenant's Woman

Elizabeth Gaskell
North and South

Oliver Goldsmith
She Stoops to Conquer

Graham Greene
Brighton Rock

Graham Greene
The Heart of the Matter

Graham Greene
The Power and the Glory

Willis Hall
The Long and the Short and the Tall

Thomas Hardy
Far from the Madding Crowd

Thomas Hardy
Jude the Obscure

Thomas Hardy
The Return of the Native

Thomas Hardy
Selected Poems

Thomas Hardy
Tess of the d'Urbervilles

L.P. Hartley
The Go-Between

Nathaniel Hawthorne
The Scarlet Letter

Seamus Heaney
Selected Poems

Ernest Hemingway
A Farewell to Arms

Ernest Hemingway
The Old Man and the Sea

Homer
The Iliad

Homer
The Odyssey

Gerard Manley Hopkins
Selected Poems

Ted Hughes
Selected Poems

Aldous Huxley
Brave New World

Henry James
Portrait of a Lady

Ben Jonson
The Alchemist

Ben Jonson
Volpone

James Joyce
A Portrait of the Artist as a Young Man

John Keats
Selected Poems

Philip Larkin
Selected Poems

D.H. Lawrence
The Rainbow

D.H. Lawrence
Selected Stories

D.H. Lawrence
Sons and Lovers

D.H. Lawrence
Women in Love

Louise Lawrence
Children of the Dust

Laurie Lee
Cider with Rosie

Christopher Marlowe
Doctor Faustus

John Milton
Paradise Lost Bks I & II

John Milton
Paradise Lost IV & IX

Robert O'Brien
Z for Zachariah

Sean O'Casey
Juno and the Paycock

George Orwell
Nineteen Eighty-four

John Osborne
Look Back in Anger

Wilfred Owen
Selected Poems

Harold Pinter
The Caretaker

Sylvia Plath
Selected Works

Alexander Pope
Selected Poems

Jean Rhys
Wide Sargasso Sea

Willy Russell
Educating Rita

Willy Russell
Our Day Out

William Shakespeare
As You Like It

William Shakespeare
Coriolanus

William Shakespeare
Henry IV Pt 1

William Shakespeare
Henry IV Pt II

William Shakespeare
Henry V

William Shakespeare
Julius Caesar

William Shakespeare
Measure for Measure

William Shakespeare
A Midsummer Night's Dream

William Shakespeare
Richard II

William Shakespeare
Richard III

William Shakespeare
Sonnets

William Shakespeare
The Taming of the Shrew

William Shakespeare
The Tempest

William Shakespeare
The Winter's Tale

George Bernard Shaw
Arms and the Man

George Bernard Shaw
Saint Joan

Richard Brinsley Sheridan
The Rivals

R.C. Sherriff
Journey's End

Rukshana Smith
Salt on the Snow

Muriel Spark
The Prime of Miss Jean Brodie

John Steinbeck
The Grapes of Wrath

John Steinbeck
The Pearl

R.L. Stevenson
Dr Jekyll and Mr Hyde

Tom Stoppard
Rosencrantz and Guildenstern are Dead

Jonathan Swift
Gulliver's Travels

Robert Swindells
Daz 4 Zoe

John Millington Synge
The Playboy of the Western World

W.M. Thackeray
Vanity Fair

Mark Twain
Huckleberry Finn

Virgil
The Aeneid

Derek Walcott
Selected Poems

Oscar Wilde
The Importance of Being Earnest

Tennessee Williams
Cat on a Hot Tin Roof

Tennessee Williams
The Glass Menagerie

Virginia Woolf
Mrs Dalloway

Virginia Woolf
To the Lighthouse

William Wordsworth
Selected Poems

W.B. Yeats
Selected Poems

Six Women Poets